Fun Facts & Trivia
1941 - A Year In Review

ISBN: 9798568273257

INDEX

FIRST EDITION

1941

January

M	T	W	T	F	S	S
		1	2	3	4	5
6	7	8	9	10	11	12
13	14	15	16	17	18	19
20	21	22	23	24	25	26
27	28	29	30	31		

◐:5 ○:13 ◑:20 ●:27

February

M	T	W	T	F	S	S
					1	2
3	4	5	6	7	8	9
10	11	12	13	14	15	16
17	18	19	20	21	22	23
24	25	26	27	28		

◐:4 ○:12 ◑:18 ●:26

March

M	T	W	T	F	S	S
					1	2
3	4	5	6	7	8	9
10	11	12	13	14	15	16
17	18	19	20	21	22	23
24	25	26	27	28	29	30
31						

◐:6 ○:13 ◑:20 ●:27

April

M	T	W	T	F	S	S
	1	2	3	4	5	6
7	8	9	10	11	12	13
14	15	16	17	18	19	20
21	22	23	24	25	26	27
28	29	30				

◐:5 ○:11 ◑:18 ●:26

May

M	T	W	T	F	S	S
			1	2	3	4
5	6	7	8	9	10	11
12	13	14	15	16	17	18
19	20	21	22	23	24	25
26	27	28	29	30	31	

◐:4 ○:11 ◑:18 ●:26

June

M	T	W	T	F	S	S
						1
2	3	4	5	6	7	8
9	10	11	12	13	14	15
16	17	18	19	20	21	22
23	24	25	26	27	28	29
30						

◐:2 ○:9 ◑:16 ●:24

July

M	T	W	T	F	S	S
	1	2	3	4	5	6
7	8	9	10	11	12	13
14	15	16	17	18	19	20
21	22	23	24	25	26	27
28	29	30	31			

◐:2 ○:8 ◑:16 ●:24 ◐:31

August

M	T	W	T	F	S	S
				1	2	3
4	5	6	7	8	9	10
11	12	13	14	15	16	17
18	19	20	21	22	23	24
25	26	27	28	29	30	31

○:7 ◑:15 ●:22 ◐:29

September

M	T	W	T	F	S	S
1	2	3	4	5	6	7
8	9	10	11	12	13	14
15	16	17	18	19	20	21
22	23	24	25	26	27	28
29	30					

○:5 ◑:13 ●:21 ◐:27

October

M	T	W	T	F	S	S
		1	2	3	4	5
6	7	8	9	10	11	12
13	14	15	16	17	18	19
20	21	22	23	24	25	26
27	28	29	30	31		

○:5 ◑:13 ●:20 ◐:27

November

M	T	W	T	F	S	S
					1	2
3	4	5	6	7	8	9
10	11	12	13	14	15	16
17	18	19	20	21	22	23
24	25	26	27	28	29	30

○:4 ◑:12 ●:19 ◐:25

December

M	T	W	T	F	S	S
1	2	3	4	5	6	7
8	9	10	11	12	13	14
15	16	17	18	19	20	21
22	23	24	25	26	27	28
29	30	31				

○:3 ◑:11 ●:18 ◐:25

PEOPLE IN HIGH OFFICE

Monarch - King George VI

Reign: 11th December 1936 - 6th February 1952

Predecessor: Edward VIII

Successor: Elizabeth II

United Kingdom
Prime Minister

Winston Churchill - Conservative
10th May 1940 - 26th July 1945

Ireland

Taoiseach Of Ireland
Éamon de Valera
Fianna Fáil
29th December 1937
- 18th February 1948

Canada

Prime Minister
Mackenzie King
Liberal Party
23rd October 1935
- 15th November 1948

United States

President
Franklin D. Roosevelt
Democratic Party
4th March 1933
- 12th April 1945

Australia	Prime Minister Robert Menzies (1939-1941) Arthur Fadden (1941) John Curtin (1941-1945)
Brazil	President Getúlio Vargas (1930-1945)
China	Premier Chiang Kai-shek (1939-1945)
Cuba	President Fulgencio Batista (1940-1944)
Egypt	Prime Minister Hussein Sirri Pasha (1940-1942)
France	President *Vacant (1940-1944)*
Germany	Chancellor Adolf Hitler (1933-1945)
India	Viceroy of India Victor Alexander John Hope (1936-1943)

Italy	Prime Minister Benito Mussolini (1922-1943)
Japan	Prime Minister Fumimaro Konoe (1940-1941) Hideki Tōjō (1941-1944)
Mexico	President Manuel Ávila Camacho (1940-1946)
New Zealand	Prime Minister Peter Fraser (1940-1949)
Russia	Communist Party Leader Joseph Stalin (1922-1952)
South Africa	Prime Minister Jan Smuts (1939-1948)
Spain	Prime Minister Francisco Franco (1938-1973)
Turkey	Prime Minister Refik Saydam (1939-1942)

BRITISH NEWS & EVENTS

JAN

3rd | Australian and British troops defeat Italian forces at the Battle of Bardia in Libya. The battle takes place between the 3rd and 5th January and is the first British military operation of the Western Desert Campaign of WW2.

9th January: The Avro Manchester Mark III BT308 (a prototype of the Avro Lancaster heavy bomber) is flown by test pilot H. A. 'Sam' Brown on its maiden flight at RAF Ringway in Cheshire. *Interesting facts: The Lancaster Bomber became one of the most heavily used of the Second World War night bombers, delivering 608,612 long tons of bombs during 156,000 sorties. The versatility of the Lancaster was such that it was chosen to equip 617 Squadron and was modified to carry the Upkeep 'Bouncing bomb' designed by Barnes Wallis for Operation Chastise, the attack on German Ruhr valley dams in May 1943. Photo: The prototype Avro Manchester Mark III Reg: BT308 in 1941.*

11th | The British Royal Navy light cruiser HMS Southampton is sunk off Malta after coming under attack from 12 Luftwaffe Stuka dive bombers; 81 men are killed as a result of the attack.

14th | In a BBC radio broadcast from London, Victor de Laveleye asks all Belgians to use the letter V as a rallying sign, being the first letter of victoire (victory) in French and of vrijheid (freedom) in Dutch. This is the beginning of the V campaign and introduces the use of the V sign for victory and freedom.

19th | British troops attack Italian-held Eritrea.

21st | The Daily Worker, the newspaper of the Communist Party of Great Britain, is suppressed by the Labour Home Secretary Herbert Morrison (until September 1942) in view of its continuing pro-Soviet stance.

JAN

21st | Australian and British forces attack and capture the Libyan city of Tobruk from the Italians (21st - 22nd January).

31st | German spy Josef Jakobs parachutes into the village of Ramsey in Cambridgeshire, breaking his ankle in the process. The following morning Jakobs is apprehended by members of the local Home Guard after being notified of his whereabouts by farmers Charles Baldock and Harry Coulson. He was caught still wearing his flying suit and carrying £500 in British currency, forged identity papers, a radio transmitter and a German sausage. *Follow up: Jakobs became last person to be executed at the Tower of London (15th August 1941) after being convicted of espionage under the Treachery Act 1940; he was shot by a military firing squad.*

FEB

5th | The Air Training Corps (ATC) is officially established with King George VI as its Air Commodore-in-Chief. The new ATC's purpose is to provide training programmes to young men who might later join the Royal Air Force.

9th | Winston Churchill makes a speech (broadcast by the BBC) asking the United States to show its support by sending arms to Britain. He ends the speech with an explicit message to President Roosevelt, "Give us the tools, and we will finish the job".

11th | RMS Queen Elizabeth leaves Singapore after a refit and begins her first voyage as a troopship. *Interesting facts: During her war service the Queen Elizabeth carried more than 750,000 troops and sailed some 500,000 miles.*

12th | Terminally ill Police Constable Albert Alexander, a patient at the Radcliffe Infirmary in Oxford, becomes the first person treated with penicillin intravenously. Alexander reacts positively to the drug but due to an insufficient supply he eventually relapses and dies on the 15th March 1941. *Follow up: A successful treatment was achieved 3 months later by Dr Howard Walter Florey and biochemist Ernst Boris Chain. They were responsible for making an effective drug out of penicillin, and alongside Sir Alexander Fleming shared the Nobel Prize in Physiology or Medicine in 1945. It is estimated that their discoveries have to date saved over 200 million lives.*

19th | The start of a three-night Blitz over Swansea, South Wales occurs resulting in 230 deaths and 397 injuries. Swansea's town centre is almost completely obliterated by the 1,273 high explosive bombs and 56,000 Incendiary bombs estimated to have been dropped by the Luftwaffe.

25th | The British submarine HMS Upright torpedoes the Italian cruiser Armando Diaz off the island of Kerkennah on the east coast of Tunisia. The ship takes only six minutes to sink after her magazine blows up; 484 men are killed in the explosion.

MAR

1st | John Gilbert Winant is appointed as United States Ambassador to the United Kingdom in succession to Joseph P. Kennedy; he remains in the post until his resignation in March 1946.

7th | Prime Minister Winston Churchill diverts 58,000 British and Australian troops from Egypt to occupy the Olympus-Vermion line in Greece.

MAR

11th U.S. President Franklin D. Roosevelt signs the Lend-Lease Act into law allowing the country to supply military equipment to Britain (and its foreign allies) whilst still remaining officially neutral.

11th Luftwaffe air raids on Manchester cause extensive damage to the city. One notable casualty is Old Trafford football stadium, the home of Manchester United F.C., which sees its stands demolished and its pitch wrecked. *Follow up: The stadium was rebuilt after the war and reopened in August 1949. During this time United played at Maine Road, the home of their cross-town rivals Manchester City, at a cost of £5,000 a year plus a percentage of the gate receipts.*

13th March: Clydebank Blitz: Over two nights Clydebank is the target of one of the most intense Luftwaffe bombing raids of World War II. Each night over 200 German bombers attack aiming to destroy naval, shipbuilding and munitions targets. Clydebank's housing bears the brunt of the raids and of its 12,000 homes only 7 properties are left undamaged (4,000 are completely destroyed). The official death toll records 528 casualties; 617 more are seriously injured and 35,000 are made homeless. *Photo: A destroyed tram surrounded by the rubble on Dumbarton Road after the Clydebank Blitz.*

17th Minister of Labour Ernest Bevin makes a call for women to fill vital jobs in industry and the Auxiliary Services (in December 1941 women begin to be conscripted for war work when Parliament passes the National Service Act).

MAR

27th | Battle of Cape Matapan: Following the interception of Italian signals by the Government Code and Cypher School at Bletchley Park, ships of the Royal Navy and Royal Australian Navy intercept and sink several ships of the Italian Regia Marina off the Peloponnesus coast in the Mediterranean. Over 2,300 Italians lose their lives and 1,015 are taken as prisoners of war in what is Italy's greatest ever defeat at sea.

29th | The first performance of British composer Benjamin Britten's Requiem Symphony takes place at Carnegie Hall, New York.

APR

Birmingham Accident Hospital and Rehabilitation Centre opens as the world's first trauma centre (using the existing buildings of Queen's Hospital in Bath Row, Birmingham).

15th | Two hundred bombers of the Luftwaffe attack military and manufacturing targets in the city of Belfast. Some 900 people die as a result of the bombings and 1,500 are injured (other than London, this is the greatest loss of life in any night raid during the Blitz).

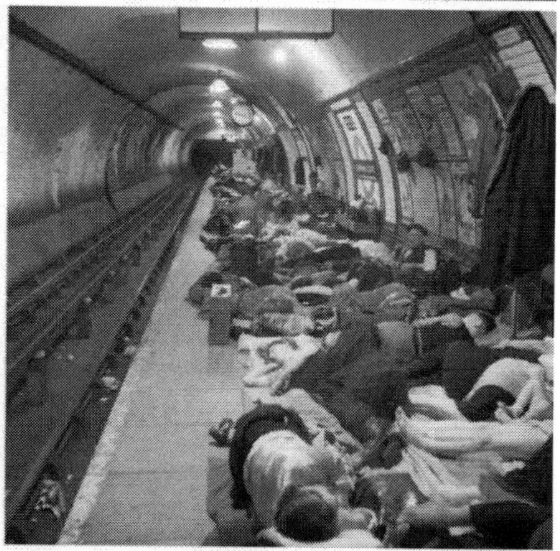

19th April: The heaviest air-raids of the year take place on London; 1,000 tons of high explosive and 153,000 incendiaries are dropped killing 1,200 people. *Facts: London was targeted a total of 71 times by the Luftwaffe's bombing campaign during the Blitz. During these raids 32,000 civilians in London were killed and 87,000 seriously injured.*

APR

21st | After the surrender of the Greek forces in Albania to the Germans the previous day, the final decision for the evacuation of Commonwealth forces from Greece, to Crete and Egypt, is taken.

22nd | The Portland Square air raid shelter in Plymouth is struck during bombing; 76 people are killed, the greatest civilian loss of life in the Plymouth Blitz.

26th | The Official recipe for Woolton Pie is reported in The Times. The pie is the invention of Francis Latry, the head chef at the Savoy Hotel in London, and is named after the Minister of Food, Lord Woolton. *Fun fact: The pie contained no meat and was one of many recipes introduced to the British people by the Ministry of Food to ensure that a nutritional diet could be maintained despite food shortages.*

MAY

1st | A seven-night bombardment by the Luftwaffe on Liverpool, the largest port on the west coast and being of significant importance to the British war effort, devastates the city. *Follow up: The sustained heavy bombing on Merseyside during the 'May Blitz' was carried out by 681 bombers and put 69 out of 144 cargo berths out of action. The raids demolished 4,400 homes in Liverpool and damaged a further 61,900; over 75,000 people on Merseyside were left homeless. By the end of the seven nights 1453 people had been killed in Liverpool, 257 in Bootle, 28 in Birkenhead and 3 in Wallasey.*

2nd | British combat operations against the rebel government of Rashid Ali, who had seized power with assistance from Germany and Italy, begin in the Kingdom of Iraq. *Follow up: The campaign results in the downfall of Ali's government on the 31st May 1941, the re-occupation of Iraq, and the return to power of the Regent of Iraq, Prince 'Abd al-Ilah, an ally to the United Kingdom.*

6th | Greenock in Scotland is intensively bombed by the Luftwaffe who target the shipyards and berthed ships around the town. Over two nights 271 people are killed and over 10,200 injured. From a total of 180,000 homes nearly 25,000 suffer damage and 5,000 are destroyed outright.

9th | The German submarine U-110 is captured by the Royal Navy in the North Atlantic after being forced to surface by depth charges. On board is the latest Enigma cryptography machine (and the U-boat's code books) which Allied cryptographers later use to break coded German messages.

10th | The House of Commons is damaged by incendiary bombs dropped by the Luftwaffe; the Commons Chamber is entirely destroyed by fire.

10th | London's Queen's Hall, the venue for The Proms, is bombed by the Luftwaffe. The concert series relocates to the Royal Albert Hall (which today remains their principal venue).

10th | Rudolf Hess parachutes into Scotland at Floors Farm, Eaglesham, south of Glasgow. He is discovered still struggling with his parachute by local ploughman David McLean who contacts the local Home Guard unit. They escort their captive to their headquarters in Busby, East Renfrewshire. Hess says he has an important message for the Duke of Hamilton and claims to be on a peace mission.

15th | The first British jet-engined aircraft, the prototype Gloster E.28/39 (also referred to as the Gloster Whittle or Gloster Pioneer) is flown for the first time at RAF Cranwell in Lincolnshire by Flight Lieutenant Gerry Sayer.

MAY

24th May: In the Battle of the Denmark Strait the German battleship Bismarck sinks the pride of the Royal Navy, the battlecruiser HMS Hood. Hood was struck near her aft ammunition magazines, and sank within 3 minutes with the loss of all but 3 of the 1418 men aboard. *Photo: HMS Hood (1924) - the last battlecruiser built for the Royal Navy.*

24th	Off the coast of Sicily, the British submarine HMS Upholder torpedoes and sinks the Italian ocean liner turned troopship SS Conte Rosso. Of the 2,729 soldiers and crew aboard, 1,300 were killed.
27th	In the Atlantic, approximately 350 miles west of Brest, France, a severely damaged Bismarck, which had been relentlessly pursued by the Royal Navy since the sinking of HMS Hood, is scuttled with heavy loss of life. Out of a crew of over 2,200 men only 114 survived (British warships rescued 111 of the survivors from Bismarck).

JUN

1st	Arthur 'Bomber' Harris is promoted to the acting rank of air marshal. *Follow up: Harris would eventually go on to become the Marshal of the Royal Air Force (1st January 1946), the highest rank in the British Royal Air Force.*
1st	Oliver Lyttleton, President of the Board of Trade, announces the introduction of clothes rationing. The news comes as a complete surprise to most people but was needed to reduce production and consumption of civilian clothes, and to safeguard raw materials and release workers (and factory space) for war production. *Further information: Clothes rationing went on until the 15th March 1949 during which time people were urged to "Make do and mend". Everyone received a Clothing Book with 60 coupons (children were allocated an extra 10 coupons) which allowed them to buy one completely new set of clothes a year.*
8th	The British and Free French forces invade Syria and Lebanon.
22nd	Operation Barbarossa: Nazi Germany and its allies invades the Soviet Union. Winston Churchill promises all possible British assistance to the Soviet Union in a worldwide broadcast: "Any man or state who fights against Nazidom will have our aid. Any man or state who marches with Hitler is our foe."

JUL

The British Army's Special Air Service is formed by David Stirling (originally called "L" Detachment, Special Air Service Brigade).

2nd Noël Coward's comic play Blithe Spirit premieres at the Piccadilly Theatre in the West End of London. *Fun fact: The play's run of 1,997 consecutive performances set a record for a non-musical play in the West End (the run was eventually surpassed by Agatha Christie's The Mousetrap in 1957).*

5th The British troopship SS Anselm is torpedoed and sunk by the German submarine U-96 in the Atlantic Ocean; 250 of the 1,310 on men onboard were lost.

7th Neutral American forces take over the defence of Iceland from the British.

12th The Anglo-Soviet Agreement is signed by the United Kingdom and the Soviet Union against Germany. Both powers pledge to assist each other and not make separate peace with Germany.

15th The MAUD Report (edited by James Chadwick) is approved and concludes an atomic bomb is feasible. *Follow up: The report was presented by Vannevar Bush to President Roosevelt in October 1941 and inspired the U.S. government to pour millions of dollars into the pursuit of an atomic bomb.*

19th July: Winston Churchill launches his "V for Victory" campaign buoyed by the success of Victor de Laveleye's call (on the 14th January) for the use the letter V as a rallying sign. The BBC also sets out a plan for the campaign and puts assistant news editor Douglas Ritchie, posing as "Colonel Britton", in charge.

23rd An Italian Savoia-Marchetti SM.79 bomber aircraft torpedoes and damages the British destroyer HMS Fearless (the detonation kills 27 and wounds 11 of the crew). Fearless cannot be saved and is sunk 58 miles north of Bône, Algeria.

AUG

	The Political Warfare Executive is formed to disseminate information to Germany and its occupied countries.
9th	Winston Churchill, onboard HMS Prince of Wales, reaches Naval Station Argentia in Newfoundland for talks with President Roosevelt. The Atlantic Charter, setting out American and British goals for the period following the end of World War II, is agreed as a result.

9th August: RAF pilot Douglas Bader, on an offensive patrol over the French coast, is forced to bale out after a mid-air collision and is taken prisoner by the Germans. *Follow up: Despite having lost both his legs in a flying accident in 1931, Bader made a number of escape attempts and was eventually sent to the prisoner of war camp at Colditz Castle. He remained there until April 1945 when the camp was liberated by the First United States Army. Photo: Highly decorated RAF flying ace Douglas Bader (credited with 22 aerial victories and 4 shared victories).*

16th	HMS Mercury Royal Navy Signals School and Combined Signals School opens at Leydene House near Petersfield in Hampshire.
18th	The National Fire Service (NFS) is established by the amalgamation of the wartime national Auxiliary Fire Service (AFS) and the local authority fire brigades (about 1,600 of them). *Interesting facts: The NFS existed until 1948 and at peak strength had 370,000 personnel including 80,000 women.*
25th	The Anglo-Soviet invasion of Iran (Operation Countenance), to secure Iranian oil fields and ensure Allied supply lines for the USSR, begins.
30th	The German troopships SS Bahia Laura and SS Donau are sunk by the British submarine HMS Trident of Seloen Island, Norway; 1,700 German troops are lost on the two ships.

AUG

30th | The first official 'Shetland Bus' clandestine mission, using Norwegian fishing boats between Shetland and German-occupied Norway, departs for Bergen from Hamnavoe, on the west side of Lunna Ness. Officially named the Norwegian Naval Independent Unit (NNIU), the Shetland Bus crossings would continue until the surrender of Nazi Germany on the 8th May 1945.

30th | Winston Churchill becomes the first national leader to approve a nuclear weapons programme (codename Tube Alloys).

30th | A German Lorenz cipher machine operator sends a 4,000-character message twice, from Athens to Vienna, without changing the key settings. This allows British mathematician Bill Tutte to decipher the machine's coding mechanism and becomes an important source of "Ultra" intelligence, contributing significantly to the eventual Allied victory against Germany.

SEP

17th | Rezā Shāh of Iran is forced to resign in favour of his son Mohammad Reza Pahlavi, under pressure from the United Kingdom and the Soviet Union, concluding the Anglo-Soviet invasion of Iran.

29th | The first Moscow Conference begins; U.S. representative Averell Harriman and British representative Lord Beaverbrook meet with Soviet foreign minister Vyacheslav Molotov to arrange urgent assistance for Russia.

OCT

The first Ronald Searle cartoon to feature St Trinian's School is published in the magazine Lilliput. *Interesting facts: Searle, who had been posted to Malaya with the 18th Infantry Division, had been unaware he had been published until February 1942 when he picked up an abandoned copy of Lilliput in a Singapore side street. Captured by the Japanese he became a POW in Changi Prison and in the Kwai jungle. Photos: Ronald Serle (1956) and a copy of his first St Trinian's cartoon for Lilliput.*

OCT

	U.S. President Franklin D. Roosevelt approves US$1bn in Lend-Lease aid to Britain.
1st	The New Zealand Division of the Royal Navy becomes the Royal New Zealand Navy.
31st	A fire at the H. Booth & Son clothing factory in Huddersfield kills 49, most of them women and young girls. The fire is caused by a smoker's pipe left alight inside a raincoat pocket.

NOV

1st	Politician Sir Charles Trevelyan announces that he is donating his family home, Wallington Hall, Northumberland, to the National Trust. Complete with the estate and farms, it is the first donation of its kind to the National Trust.
10th	In a speech at the Mansion House in London, Winston Churchill promises "should the United States become involved in war with Japan, the British declaration will follow within the hour."

13th November: The Royal Navy aircraft carrier HMS Ark Royal is hit by the German submarine U-81 off Gibraltar; she capsizes and sinks under tow the next day. *Photo: A listing Ark Royal hands survivors over to HMS Legion before sinking; of her crew of 1,488 there was just one fatality, Able Seaman Edward Mitchell.*

18th	Operation Crusader, a British Eighth Army operation to relieve the Siege of Tobruk in North Africa, begins. *Follow up: Tobruk is relieved by the Eighth Army on the 27th November.*
22nd	HMS Devonshire sinks the commerce raiding German auxiliary cruiser Atlantis. *Atlantis facts: During its WW2 campaign the cruiser sank or captured 22 ships (13 British), and travelled more 100,000 miles in 602 days.*

DEC

5th Britain declares war on Finland, Hungary and Romania.

6th The British submarine HMS Perseus strikes an Italian mine off Cephalonia, 7 miles north of Zakynthos in the Ionian Sea; 31-year-old leading stoker John Capes is the only survivor out of the 61 men on board. *Notes: After escaping from the submarine Capes swam 5 miles to the island of Cephalonia where he was hidden by islanders for 18 months before being smuggled to Smyrna, Turkey. He was subsequently awarded a British Empire Medal.*

8th A declaration of war by the Empire of Japan on the United States and the British Empire is published on the front page of all Japanese newspapers' evening editions. The declaration appears an hour after Japanese forces had begun their attacks on the U.S. naval base at Pearl Harbor and on British forces in Malaya, Singapore, and Hong Kong.

10th The Royal Navy ships HMS Prince of Wales and HMS Repulse are sunk by Japanese aircraft near Kuantan, in the South China Sea. They are the first capital ships to be sunk solely by air power on the open sea.

13th Britain, New Zealand, and South Africa declare war on Bulgaria.

14th The German submarine U-557 torpedoes and sinks the British light cruiser Galatea off Alexandria, Egypt. Galatea's Captain E.W.B. Sim, 22 officers and 447 ratings are killed; some 100 survivors are picked up by the destroyers Griffin and Hotspur.

18th Parliament passes the second National Service Act widening the scope of conscription still further. All unmarried women and childless widows between the ages of 20 and 30 are liable to be called-up, and men are now required to do some form of National Service up to the age of 60, including military service for those under 51.

19th Italian Regia Marina divers on human torpedoes place limpet mines on the Royal Navy Mediterranean Fleet in port at Alexandria, Egypt. The battleships Queen Elizabeth and Valiant are severely damaged in the raid.

22nd The Arcadia Conference opens in Washington, D.C., the first meeting on military strategy between the heads of government of the United Kingdom and the United States following the latter's entry into the war.

25th The Battle of Hong Kong ends after 17 days with surrender, by Governor Sir Mark Aitchison Young, of the Crown colony of Hong Kong to the Japanese.

25th Field Marshal Sir Alan Brooke succeeds Field Marshal Sir John Dill as Chief of the Imperial General Staff, an office he will hold until the 25th June 1946.

27th Winston Churchill becomes the first British Prime Minister to address a Joint session of the U.S. Congress. He ends his speech, which runs for over 30 minutes, to thunderous applause. He then flashes a V for victory sign before leaving the chamber. The New York Times describes his address as "full of bubbling humour, biting denunciation of totalitarian enemies, stern courage - and hard facts".

60 Worldwide News & Events

1. 1st January: Thailand's Prime Minister Plaek Phibunsongkhram decrees that the 1st January will now be the official start of the new year. *Note: Songkran was the official new year until 1888, after which it was switched to the 1st April.*

2. 4th January: The Merrie Melodies cartoon Elmer's Pet Rabbit is released and is the first to use Bugs Bunny's name on-screen. *Fun facts: Bugs Bunny's official debut was in A Wild Hare (1940), but the prototypical version of Bugs Bunny appeared in four cartoons before this dating back to Happy Rabbit in Porky's Hare Hunt (1938). Bugs Bunny has appeared in more films than any other cartoon character and has his own star on the Hollywood Walk of Fame. Pictured: Bugs Bunny's evolution from Happy Rabbit in 1938 to the present day.*

3. 6th January: In an address known as the Four Freedoms speech (technically the 1941 State of the Union address), President Roosevelt proposes four fundamental freedoms that people everywhere in the world ought to enjoy; 1. Freedom of speech, 2. Freedom of worship, 3. Freedom from want, 4. Freedom from fear.
4. 14th January: Commerce raiding German auxiliary cruiser Pinguin captures the Norwegian whaling fleet near Bouvet Island, effectively ending Southern Ocean whaling for the duration of the war. *Notes: Pinguin's operation against the Norwegian whaling fleet was the single most successful performance by a German auxiliary cruiser in World War II. More than 36,000 tons of shipping, a supply-ship, two factory ships, 11 whalers, 20,000 tons of whale oil with a value of over $4 million, and 10,000 tons of fuel oil were captured.*
5. 31st January: Boxer Joe Louis knocks out Red Burman in 5 rounds to retain The Ring and lineal heavyweight titles. This is the 13th defence of his titles since winning them from James J. Braddock on the 22nd June 1937, and he goes on to defend them a further 6 times in 1941 against; Gus Dorazio, Abe Simon, Tony Musto, Buddy Baer, Billy Conn, and Lou Nova. *Fun facts: In all, Louis made 25 defences of his heavyweight titles between 1937 and 1948, and was a world champion for 11 years and 10 months. His most remarkable record is that he knocked out 23 opponents in 27 title fights, including five world champions.*
6. 6th February: Lieutenant-General Erwin Rommel is appointed commander of the Afrika Korps (the German expeditionary force in Africa).

7. 23rd February: The chemical element 94, plutonium, is first synthesised by Glenn T. Seaborg, Arthur C. Wahl, Joseph W. Kennedy and Edwin McMillan at the University of California, Berkeley; it is kept secret until after the atomic bombings of Hiroshima and Nagasaki.

8. 25th February: A general strike in the German-occupied Netherlands begins in defence of persecuted Dutch Jews, and against the anti-Jewish measures and activities of the Nazis in general. *Notes: The 1941 February Strike is considered to be the first public protest against the Nazis in occupied Europe, and the only mass protest against the deportation of Jews to be organised by non-Jews.*

9. 27th February: The 13th Academy Awards, honouring the best in film in 1940, are held at the Biltmore Hotel in Los Angeles, California. The winners include Alfred Hitchcock's film Rebecca (his only film to win Best Picture), James Stewart and Ginger Rogers. Disney's Pinocchio becomes the first animated film to take home a competitive Oscar, winning for both Best Original Score and Best Original Song. *Notes: This is the first year that sealed envelopes are used to keep secret the names of the winners, leading to the famous phrase: "May I have the envelope, please?" The accounting firm of Price Waterhouse is hired to count the ballots after the fiasco of leaked voting results in 1939 by the Los Angeles Times.*

10. March: Captain America and his sidekick Bucky make their first appearance in Captain America Comics No.1, from Timely Comics, a predecessor of Marvel Comics (although cover-dated March 1941, it actually went on sale the 20th December 1940). *Fun facts: The first issue, showing the protagonist punching Nazi leader Adolf Hitler, went on to sell nearly one million copies. In August 2011 a copy of the comic (graded 9.2) sold for $343,057.*

11. 22nd March: James Stewart is inducted into the U.S. Army and becomes the first major American movie star to wear a military uniform in World War II. *Follow up: Stewart served as a pilot during World War II and was awarded two Distinguished Flying Crosses and four Air Medals. He later went on to serve in the Vietnam War, rising to the rank of brigadier general in the U.S. Air Force Reserve. Photos: Corporal Stewart is commissioned a Second Lieutenant in the U.S. Army Air Corps at Moffett Field, California (1942) / Brigadier General James Stewart (1968).*

12. April: The Valley of Geysers is discovered on Russia's Kamchatka Peninsula by Soviet geologist Tatyana Ustinova.
13. 6th April: Germany invades the Kingdom of Yugoslavia and Greece.
14. 13th April: The Soviet-Japanese Neutrality Pact is signed in Moscow.

15. 18th April: Greek Prime Minister Alexandros Koryzis commits suicide as German troops approach Athens.
16. 1st May: Orson Welles' film Citizen Kane premieres at the Palace Theatre in New York City. Starring himself, Joseph Cotten and Dorothy Corningore, the picture is Welles's first feature film.
17. 1st May: The breakfast cereal CheeriOats is introduced by American manufacturer General Mills; the cereal is renamed Cheerios in 1945.
18. 5th May: Emperor Haile Selassie enters Addis Ababa after it has been liberated from Italian forces; this date is subsequently commemorated as Liberation Day in Ethiopia.
19. 5th May: French couturier Gabrielle 'Coco' Chanel releases her first perfume, Chanel No.5.
20. 6th May: Joseph Stalin replaces Vyacheslav Molotov to become the Premier of the Soviet Union.
21. 7th May: Glenn Miller records the big band / swing tune Chattanooga Choo Choo for RCA Victor. Written by Mack Gordon and composed by Harry Warren, it features in the 1941 movie Sun Valley Serenade, and becomes the first song to receive a gold record with sales of 1.2 million copies.
22. 12th May: Konrad Zuse presents the Z3 to an audience of scientists in Berlin. It is the world's first working programmable, fully automatic computer.
23. 12th May: Martin Bormann succeeds Rudolf Hess as Adolf Hitler's deputy.
24. 25th May: 5,000 people drown in a storm in the Ganges Delta region of India.
25. 1st June: The Battle of Crete ends as Crete surrenders to invading German forces.
26. 5th June: Around 4,000 Chongqing residents are asphyxiated in a tunnel during the bombing of Chongqing, China, by the Japanese.
27. 18th June: The German-Turkish Treaty of Friendship is signed between Nazi Germany and Turkey, in Ankara.
28. 25th June: Finland (as a co-belligerent with Germany) attacks the Soviet Union to start the Continuation War.
29. 28th June: The U.S. Office of Scientific Research and Development is created with Vannevar Bush as its director. It is charged with research into a wide variety of projects, one of which would be the secret S-1 Section whose work into the development the first atomic weapons provided the groundwork for the Manhattan Project.
30. 30th June: The massacres (pogroms) of thousands of Jews by Ukrainian nationalists, Nazi SS paramilitary death squads (Einsatzgruppen), and local crowds, begin in the city of Lwów (now Lviv, Ukraine).
31. 5th July: A border war, known locally as the War of '41, begins between Peru and Ecuador; a ceasefire agreement between the two countries is reached on the 31st July 1941.
32. 19th July: The MGM cartoon, The Midnight Snack, by William Hanna and Joseph Barbera, is released and features the second appearance of Tom and Jerry. *Fun facts: It is the first cartoon in which the duo are officially named. They had previously appeared in Puss Gets the Boot (1940), but had been called Jasper (Tom) and Jinx (Jerry).*
33. 31st July: The Holocaust: Under instructions from Adolf Hitler, Nazi official Hermann Göring orders S.S. General Reinhard Heydrich to work out the plan of the Final Solution of the Jewish Problem (i.e. the deliberate and systematic extermination of all Jewish people).
34. 6th August: Six-year-old Elaine Esposito undergoes an appendectomy and lapses into a coma that lasts for a record-breaking 37 years; Edwarda O'Bara and Aruna Shanbaug later exceeded Esposito's record, both spent 42 years in a coma.

35. 21st August: In revenge for the execution two days earlier of French Resistance member Samuel Tyszelman, communist activist Pierre Georges (and three companions) shoot German soldier Alfons Moser in occupied Paris; Moser's death initiates a cycle of assassinations and retribution that results in 500 French hostages being executed over the following months.

36. 28th August: German troops capture Tallinn, Estonia from the Soviet Union. Attacks on the evacuating Soviet ships leave more than 12,400 dead in one of the bloodiest naval battles of the war.

37. 29th August: Robert Menzies resigns as Prime Minister of Australia after losing the support of his party. Arthur Fadden, leader of the Country Party, consequently becomes Prime Minister, while former Prime Minister Billy Hughes replaces Menzies as UAP leader. *Follow up: Menzies subsequently helps to create the new Liberal Party and is elected its inaugural leader in August 1945. At the 1949 federal election he leads the Liberal-Country coalition to victory and returns as prime minister, a position he holds until the 26th January 1966.*

38. 1st September: The Messerschmitt Me 163 Komet, a German rocket-powered interceptor aircraft designed by Alexander Lippisch, is flown for the first time. *Interesting facts: The Komet is the only rocket-powered fighter aircraft ever to have been operational and is the first piloted aircraft of any type to exceed 1000 km/h (621 mph) in level flight. Photo: A Messerschmitt Me163b, circa 1944.*

39. 1st September: A decree issued and signed by German SS officer Reinhard Heydrich requires all Jews over the age of six, in the Reich and the Protectorate of Bohemia and Moravia, to wear a yellow Star of David with the word Jude (German for Jew) inscribed within it on their outer clothing. The practice is gradually introduced in other German-occupied areas using local words (e.g., Juif in France, Jood in the Netherlands).

40. 8th September: A siege of the Soviet city of Leningrad (now Saint Petersburg) by German troops begins. *Notes: The Siege of Leningrad was one of the deadliest and most destructive sieges in the history of the world. It would last for 872 days and would lead to more than 2,000,000 Soviet civilian and military casualties, as well as 580,000 German casualties.*

41. 11th September: Construction of the Pentagon (the headquarters of the U.S. Department of Defense) begins in Arlington County, Virginia. Designed by architect George Bergstrom, the Pentagon is officially opened on the 14th January 1943 (although the buildings first employees moved in on the 30th April 1942). *Interesting facts: The Pentagon is the world's largest office building with about 600,000m^2 of space, and has 23,000 military and civilian employees, and another 3,000 non-defence support personnel.*

42. 27th September: The National Liberation Front (Greece) (the main Greek Resistance movement) is established, and Georgios Siantos is appointed its first acting leader.

43. 27th September: The first Liberty ship, the SS Patrick Henry, is launched from the U.S. city of Baltimore, Maryland. *Interesting facts: Liberty ships were a class of cargo ship that was developed to meet British orders for transports to replace ships that had been lost. American shipyards built 2,710 Liberty ships between 1941 and 1945, the largest number of ships ever produced to a single design. Photo: The Patrick Henry being launched at the Bethlehem-Fairfield Shipyard in Baltimore.*

44. 29th-30th September: German forces, under the command of SS-Standartenführer Paul Blobel, massacre 33,771 Jews at Babi Yar in the Ukrainian capital Kiev.
45. 2nd October: Operation Typhoon begins as Germany launches an all-out offensive against Moscow.
46. 7th October: John Curtin becomes the 14th Prime Minister of Australia following the defeat of Arthur Fadden's Country / UAP Coalition Government.
47. 17th October: General Hideki Tōjō becomes the 40th Prime Minister of Japan.
48. 22nd-24th October: Romanian soldiers, German Einsatzgruppe SS and local ethnic Germans massacre some 25,000 to 34,000 Jews in the city of Odessa in Ukraine.

49. 31st October: After 14 years, work ceases on sculpting Mount Rushmore National Memorial in the U.S. town of Keystone, South Dakota. *Fun facts: Sculpted by Gutzon Borglum and 400 workers, the colossal 60-foot-high carvings of Presidents George Washington, Thomas Jefferson, Theodore Roosevelt, and Abraham Lincoln were carved to represent the first 130 years of American history. Today Mount Rushmore is South Dakota's top tourist attraction bringing in around three million tourists every year from all over the world.*

50. 7th November: Soviet leader Joseph Stalin delivers an historic address in which he claims that, in 4 months of war, Germany has lost 4.5 million soldiers (a gross exaggeration), and that a Soviet victory is near.
51. 7th November: The Soviet hospital ship Armenia is sunk by German aircraft while evacuating civilians and wounded soldiers from Crimea; it has been estimated that approximately 5,000 to 7,000 people were killed during the sinking, making it one of the deadliest maritime disasters in history. There were only 8 survivors.
52. 19th November: A battle between the Australian cruiser HMAS Sydney and German auxiliary cruiser Kormoran takes place off the coast of Western Australia. The Sydney sinks with the loss of all hands (645), and the Kormoran is scuttled due to damage sustained during the battle; 318 of the 399 crew aboard the German ship are rescued and placed in prisoner of war camps for the duration of World War II.
53. 26th November: A task force of 6 aircraft carriers, commanded by Japanese Vice Admiral Chūichi Nagumo, leaves Hitokapu Bay for Pearl Harbor, under strict radio silence.

54. 30th November and 8th December: Nazi Einsatzgruppe SS, with the help of local collaborators, kill 25,000 Jews in or on the way to Rumbula forest near Riga, Latvia.

55. December: Wonder Woman makes her first appearance in All Star Comics No.8 (the comic was actually released in October 1941 but was cover dated December 1941 / January 1942).

56. 7th December: The Imperial Japanese Navy launch a surprise, pre-emptive military strike on the U.S. Navy fleet at Pearl Harbor. The base is attacked by 353 Imperial Japanese aircraft launched in two waves from its six aircraft carriers. *Casualties and losses: As a result of the attack all eight Navy battleships at Pearl Harbor are damaged, with four sunk. The Japanese also damage a number of other ships including 3 cruisers and 3 destroyers. Additionally, 188 U.S. aircraft are destroyed and 159 damaged; 2,403 Americans are killed during the attack. Japanese losses include 29 aircraft and five midget submarines; 64 Japanese servicemen are killed and one is captured. Photo: USS Arizona on fire after the Imperial Japanese Navy Air Service attack on Pearl Harbor, December 7, 1941; she sank, with the loss of 1,177 officers and crewmen.*

57. 8th December: President Roosevelt delivers his famous "Infamy Speech", and within an hour Congress passes a formal declaration of war against Japan.

58. 11th December: Japan's allies, Germany and Italy, declare war on the United States; the U.S. responds in kind.

59. 13th December: Sweden's lowest ever temperature of -53°C is recorded in the village of Malgovik, Lappland.

60. 24th December: The Dutch submarine HNLMS K XVI becomes the first Allied submarine to sink a Japanese warship after it torpedoes the Japanese destroyer Sagiri. The following day HNLMS K XVI is itself torpedoed by the Japanese submarine I-66 (later renumbered to be I-166) off Borneo; all 36 aboard are killed.

BIRTHS

BRITISH PERSONALITIES

BORN IN 1941

Graham Chapman

b. 8th January 1941

d. 4th October 1989

Comedian, writer, actor, author and member of comedy group Monty Python.

Michael Apted, CMG

b. 10th February 1941

Director, producer, writer and actor.

Paddy Ashdown, GCMG, CH, KBE, PC

b. 27th February 1941

d. 22nd December 2018

Politician and diplomat who served as Leader of the Liberal Democrats.

Bill Tarmey

b. 4th April 1941

d. 9th November 2012

Actor, singer and author known for playing Jack Duckworth in Coronation Street.

Gordon Kaye
b. 7th April 1941
d. 23rd January 2017
Actor and singer best known for playing René Artois in 'Allo 'Allo!

Cornelia Frances, OAM
b. 7th April 1941
d. 28th May 2018
British-Australian actress.

Vivienne Westwood, DBE, RDI
b. 8th April 1941

Fashion designer and businesswoman.

Bobby Moore, OBE
b. 12th April 1941
d. 24th February 1993
Footballer who was captain of the England team that won the 1966 FIFA World Cup.

Ed 'Stewpot' Stewart
b. 23rd April 1941
d. 9th January 2016
Broadcaster known for his work as a DJ on BBC Radio and as a presenter on BBC TV.

Eric Burdon
b. 11th May 1941

Singer-songwriter and actor who sang with the rock band the Animals.

Joe Brown, MBE

b. 13th May 1941

Entertainer who has worked as a singer and guitarist for more than six decades.

Miriam Margolyes, OBE

b. 18th May 1941

British-Australian actress and voice artist.

Ming Campbell, CH, CBE, PC, QC, Kt

b. 22nd May 1941

Politician, advocate and former athlete who served as Leader of the Liberal Democrats.

Charlie Watts

b. 2nd June 1941

Drummer with Rolling Stones since 1963.

Mike Yarwood, OBE

b. 14th June 1941

Impressionist, comedian and actor.

Delia Smith, CH, CBE

b. 18th June 1941

Celebrity chef and television presenter.

Michael Howard, CH, PC, QC

b. 7th July 1941

Politician who served as Leader of the Conservative Party.

Bill Oddie, OBE

b. 7th July 1941

Writer, comedian, musician, artist, birder, conservationist, TV presenter and actor.

Craig Douglas

b. 12th August 1941

Pop singer whose career was at its greatest during the late 1950s and early 1960s.

John McNally

b. 30th August 1941

Guitarist and vocalist who was one of the original founders of The Searchers in 1957.

Sue MacGregor, CBE

b. 30th August 1941

Broadcaster best known for presenting Woman's Hour and the Today programme.

Martine Beswick

b. 26th September 1941

Actress, model and former Bond girl.

Stephanie Cole, OBE
b. 5th October 1941

Stage, television, radio and film actress.

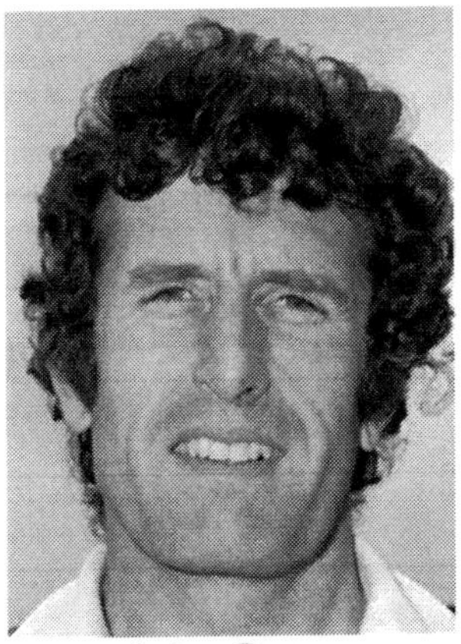

John Snow
b. 13th October 1941

Cricketer who played for Sussex and England.

Hank Marvin
b. 28th October 1941

Vocalist and songwriter best known as the lead guitarist of the Shadows.

John Pullin
b. 1st November 1941

International rugby union player.

Bruce Welch, OBE
b. 2nd November 1941

Guitarist, songwriter, producer and singer best known as a member of the Shadows.

Tom Conti
b. 22nd November 1941

Actor, theatre director and novelist.

Pete Best

b. 24th November 1941

Musician and former drummer with the Beatles.

Sir Geoff Hurst, MBE

b. 8th December 1941

Footballer who scored a hat-trick in the 1966 World Cup final.

Prince William of Gloucester

b. 18th December 1941
d. 28th August 1972

Grandson of King George V who at birth was fourth in line to the throne.

Ray Thomas

b. 29th December 1941
d. 4th January 2018

Musician, flautist, singer and founding member / composer of the Moody Blues.

Sarah Miles

b. 31st December 1941

Theatre and film actress.

Sir Alex Ferguson, CBE

b. 31st December 1941

Football manager and player noted for his time managing Manchester United.

Notable British Deaths

Amy Johnson, CBE (b. 1st July 1903; disappeared presumed dead 5th January 1941) - Pioneering English pilot who in May 1930 became the first woman to fly solo from England to Australia. Flying solo, or with her Scottish husband Jim Mollison, she set many long-distance records around the globe during the 1930s.

8th Jan	Lieutenant General Robert Stephenson Smyth Baden-Powell, 1st Baron Baden-Powell, OM, GCMG, GCVO, KCB, KStJ, DL (b. 22nd February 1857) - British Army officer, writer, founder and first Chief Scout of the world-wide Boy Scout Movement.
10th Jan	Frank Bridge (b. 26th February 1879) - Composer, violist and conductor.
12th Feb	Charles Francis Annesley Voysey (b. 28th May 1857) - Architect and furniture and textile designer.
11th Mar	Sir Henry Walford Davies, KCVO, OBE (b. 6th September 1869) - Composer, organist, conductor and educator who held the title Master of the King's Music from 1934 until 1941.
28th Mar	Adeline Virginia Woolf (b. 25th January 1882) - Writer considered one of the most important modernist 20th century authors.
5th Apr	Sir Herbert Nigel Gresley, CBE (b. 19th June 1876) - One of Britain's most famous steam locomotive engineers who rose to become Chief Mechanical Engineer of the London and North Eastern Railway.
16th Apr	Josiah Charles Stamp, 1st Baron Stamp, GCB, GBE, FBA (b. 21st June 1880) - Industrialist, economist, civil servant, statistician and writer who served as both a director of the Bank of England and chairman of the London, Midland and Scottish Railway.
17th Apr	Albert Allick Bowlly (b. 7th January 1898) - Mozambican-born, South African / British vocalist and jazz guitarist who recorded more than 1,000 songs.
7th May	Sir James George Frazer, OM, FRS, FRSE, FBA (b. 1st January 1854) - Social anthropologist and folklorist influential in the early stages of the modern studies of mythology and comparative religion.
23rd May	Herbert Austin, 1st Baron Austin, KBE (b. 8th November 1866) - Automobile designer and builder who founded the Austin Motor Company.

24th May	Vice Admiral Lancelot Ernest Holland, CB (b. 13th September 1887) - Royal Navy officer who commanded the British force in the Battle of the Denmark Strait; he was lost alongside 1414 other men when HMS Hood was sunk by the German battleship Bismarck.
1st Jun	Sir Hugh Seymour Walpole, CBE (b. 13th March 1884) - Novelist and best-selling author during the 1920s and 1930s.
15th Jun	Evelyn Underhill (b. 6th December 1875) - Anglo-Catholic writer and pacifist known for her numerous works on religion and spiritual practice.
11th Jul	Sir Arthur John Evans, FRS, FBA, FREng (b. 8th July 1851) - Archaeologist and pioneer in the study of Aegean civilization in the Bronze Age. Evans is most famous for unearthing the palace of Knossos on the Greek island of Crete.
29th Jul	James Albert Stephenson (b. 14th April 1889) - Stage and film actor.
12th Aug	Robert Peel (b. 12th February 1857) - Cricketer who played for Yorkshire and represented England in 20 Test matches.

David Devant (b. 22nd February 1868 - d. 13th October 1941) - Magician, shadowgraphist and film exhibitor who was the first President of The Magic Circle. Devant is regarded by magicians as a consummate exponent of suave and witty presentation of stage illusion. Magic historian Jim Steinmeyer describes him as "England's greatest magician and arguably the greatest magician of the 20th century".

20th Oct	Kenneth Farnes (b. 8th July 1911) - Cricketer and RAF Volunteer Reserve pilot. Farnes played in 15 Tests matches for England between 1934 and 1939.
7th Nov	Frank Pick, Hon. RIBA (b. 23rd November 1878) - Transport administrator who was the chief executive officer and vice-chairman of the London Passenger Transport Board from its creation in 1933 until 1940.
7th Dec	Cecil Forsyth (b. 30th November 1870) - Composer and musicologist.

POPULAR MUSIC

Glenn Miller & His Orchestra	No.1	Chattanooga Choo Choo
The Ink Spots	No.2	We Three (My Echo, My Shadow & Me)
Jimmy Dorsey	No.3	Maria Elena
Bing Crosby	No.4	Dolores
The Ink Spots	No.5	I Don't Want To Set The World On Fire
Dinah Shore	No.6	Yes My Darling Daughter
Bing Crosby	No.7	You Are My Sunshine
Hal Kemp & His Orchestra	No.8	So You're The One
The Andrews Sisters	No.9	I'll Be With You In Apple Blossom Time
Vera Lynn	No.10	Over The Hill

N.B. During this era music was dominated by a number of 'Big Bands' and songs could be attributed to the band leader, the band name, the lead singer or a combination of these. On top of this the success of a song was tied to the sales of sheet music, so a popular song would often be perfomed by many different combinations of singers and bands, and the contemporary charts would list the song without clarifying whose version was the major hit. With this in mind although the above chart has been compiled with best intent it does remain subjective.

1 Glenn Miller & His Orchestra
Chattanooga Choo Choo

Label:	Written by:	Length:
HMV	Warren / Gordon	3 mins 31 secs

Alton Glenn Miller (b. 1st March 1904 - MIA 15th December 1944) was a big-band musician, arranger, composer and bandleader in the swing era. He was the best-selling recording artist from 1939 to 1943, leading one of the best-known big bands and scoring 23 No.1 hits. "Chattanooga Choo Choo" featured in the film Sun Valley Serenade (1941) and was the first song to receive a gold record in the U.S.

---

2 The Ink Spots
We Three (My Echo, My Shadow & Me)

Label:	Written by:	Length:
Brunswick	Robertson / Cogane / Mysels	3 mins 18 secs

The Ink Spots, Bill Kenny (b. 12th June 1914 - d. 23rd March 1978), Deek Watson (b. 18th July 1909 - d. 4th November 1969), Charlie Fuqua (b. 20th October 1910 - d. 21st December 1971), and Hoppy Jones (b. 17th February 1905 - d. 18th October 1944), were a pop vocal group who gained international fame in the 1930s and 1940s.

Jimmy Dorsey
Maria Elena

Label:	**Written by:**	**Length:**
Decca	Barcelata / Russell	3 mins 1 sec

James Francis Dorsey (b. 29th February 1904 - d. 12th June 1957) was a jazz clarinettist, saxophonist, composer and big band leader known professionally as Jimmy Dorsey. He was inducted into the Big Band Hall of Fame in 1983 and is considered one of the most important and influential alto saxophone players of the Big Band and Swing era. Dorsey notably played clarinet on the seminal jazz standards Singin' the Blues (1927) and the original recording of Georgia on My Mind (1930), both of which were inducted into the Grammy Hall of Fame.

Bing Crosby
Dolores

Label:	**Written by:**	**Length:**
Brunswick	Alter / Loesser	3 mins 15 secs

Harry Lillis 'Bing' Crosby, Jr. (b. 3rd May 1903 - d. 14th October 1977) was a singer, comedian and an Oscar winning actor who also bred racehorses and co-owned the Pittsburgh Pirates baseball team. Crosby's trademark warm bass-baritone voice made him the best-selling recording artist of the 20th century, selling close to a billion records, tapes, compact discs and digital downloads worldwide.

The Ink Spots
I Don't Want To Set The World On Fire

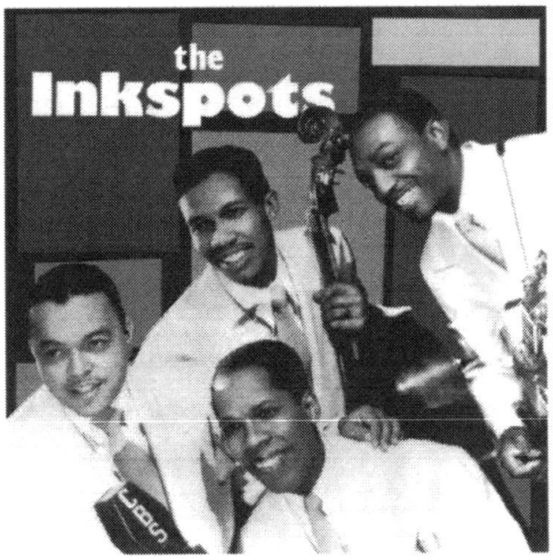

Label:	Written by:	Length:
Brunswick	Benjamin / Marcus / Durham / Seiler	2 mins 48 secs

The Ink Spots were widely accepted in both the white and black communities largely due to the ballad style introduced to the group by lead singer Bill Kenny. Since they disbanded in 1954 there have been well over 100 vocal groups calling themselves The Ink Spots without any right to the name. The original members of the group were inducted into the Rock and Roll Hall of Fame in 1989, and the Vocal Group Hall of Fame in 1999.

Dinah Shore
Yes My Darling Daughter

Label:	Written by:	Length:
Regal Zonophone	Jack Lawrence	2 mins 19 secs

Dinah Shore (b. Frances Rose Shore; 29th February 1916 - d. 24th February 1994) was a singer, actress, television personality and the top-charting female vocalist during the Big Band era of the 1940s and 1950s. After failing singing auditions for the bands of Benny Goodman, and both Jimmy Dorsey and his brother Tommy Dorsey, Shore struck out on her own and became the first singer of her era to achieve huge solo success.

7

Bing Crosby
You Are My Sunshine

Label:	**Written by:**	**Length:**
Brunswick	Davis / Mitchell	2 mins 35 secs

Bing Crosby was the first real multimedia star and was a leader in record sales, radio ratings, and motion picture grosses from 1931 to 1954. His early career coincided with recording innovations that allowed him to develop an intimate singing style that influenced many male singers who followed him including Perry Como, Frank Sinatra, Dick Haymes, and Dean Martin. For his achievements Crosby has been recognised with three stars on the Hollywood Walk of Fame; for motion pictures, radio, and audio recording.

8

Hal Kemp & His Orchestra
So You're The One

Label:	**Written by:**	**Length:**
HMV	Zaret / Whitney / Kramer	2 mins 48 secs

James Hal Kemp (b. 27th March 1904 - d. 21st December 1940) was a jazz alto saxophonist, clarinettist, bandleader, composer and arranger who was inducted into the Big Band and Jazz Hall of Fame in 1992. "So You're The One" featured a vocal refrain from the big-band singer **Janet Blair** (b. Martha Janet Lafferty; 23rd April 23, 1921 - d. 19th February 19, 2007) who went on to become a popular American film and television actress.

9 The Andrews Sisters
I'll Be With You In Apple Blossom Time

Label:	Written by:	Length:
Capitol	Tilzer / Fleeson	2 mins 58 secs

The Andrews Sisters were a close harmony singing group from the eras of swing and boogie-woogie. The group consisted of three sisters: LaVerne Sophia (b. 6th July 1911 - d. 8th May 1967), Maxene Angelyn (b. 3rd January 1916 - d. 21st October 1995) and Patricia Marie (b. 16th February 1918 - d. 30th January 2013). Throughout their long career the sisters sold well over 75 million records.

---

10 Vera Lynn
Over The Hill

Label:	Written by:	Length:
Decca	Mason	3 mins 24 secs

Dame **Vera Margaret Lynn**, CH DBE OStJ (née Welch; b. 20th March 1917) is a singer, songwriter and actress whose musical recordings and performances were enormously popular during the Second World War. Widely known as the Forces' Sweetheart, during the war she toured Egypt, India and Burma as part of ENSA, giving outdoor concerts for the troops. Lynn is the oldest person to have a No.1 album in the charts (aged 97), and became the first centenarian to have a charting album in 2017 with "Vera Lynn 100".

1941: TOP FILMS

1. **How Green Was My Valley -** *20th Century Fox*
2. **Sergeant York -** *Warner Bros.*
3. **The Maltese Falcon** - *Warner Bros.*
4. **The Little Foxes** - *RKO Radio Pictures*
5. **Citizen Kane** - *RKO Radio Pictures*

OSCARS

Best Picture: How Green Was My Valley

Most Nominations: Sergeant York (11)
Most Wins: How Green Was My Valley (5)

Best Director: John Ford - *How Green Was My Valley*

Best Actor: Gary Cooper - *Sergeant York*
Best Actress: Joan Fontaine - *Suspicion*
Best Supporting Actor: Donald Crisp - *How Green Was My Valley*
Best Supporting Actress: Mary Astor - *The Great Lie*

The 14th Academy Awards, honouring the best in film for 1941, were presented on the 26th February 1942 at the Biltmore Hotel in Los Angeles, California.

How Green Was My Valley

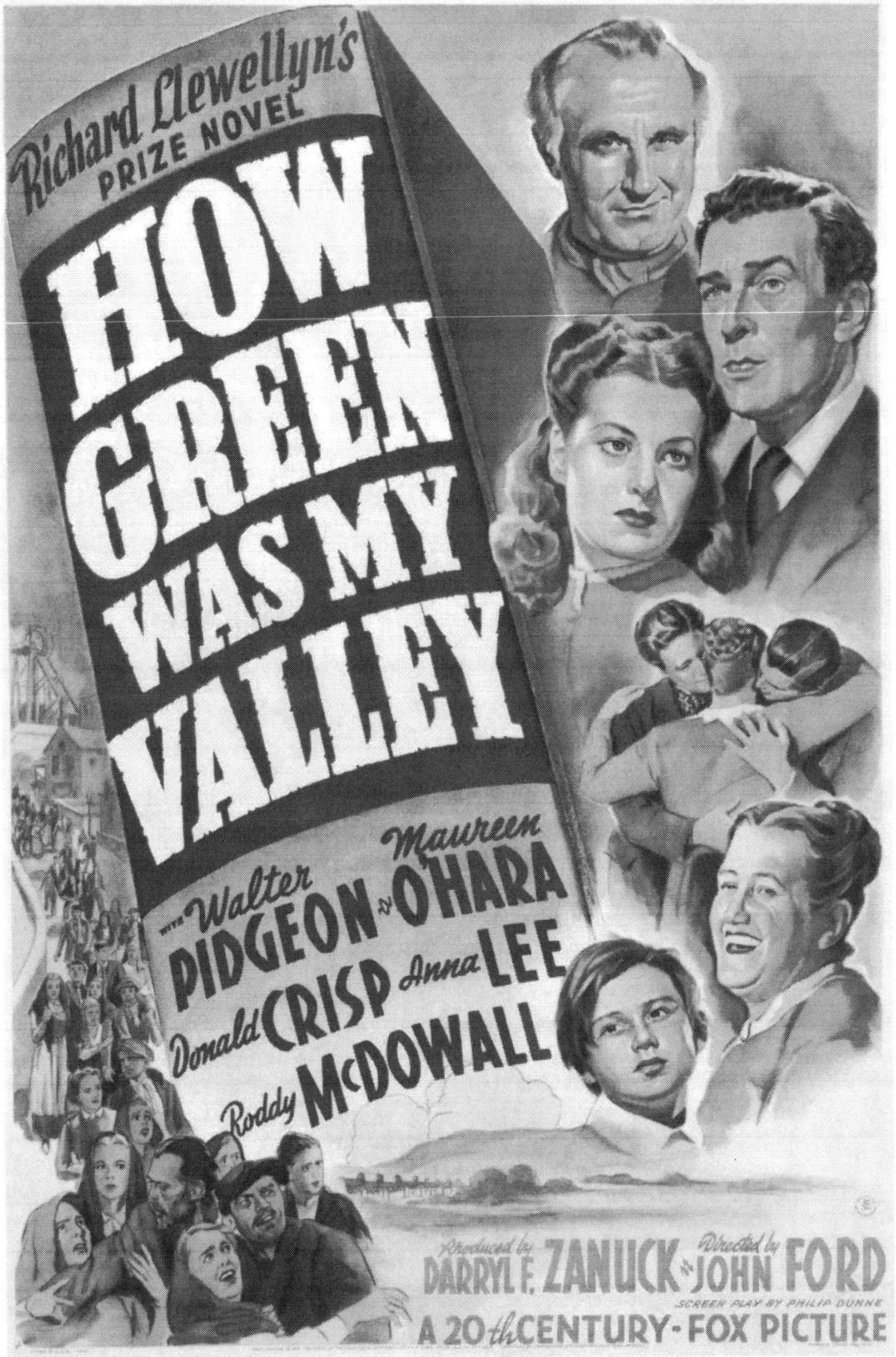

Directed by: John Ford - Runtime: 1h 58min

The story of the Morgans, a hard-working Welsh mining family during the late Victorian era, from the point of view of the youngest child Huw.

Starring

Walter Pidgeon
b. 23rd September 1897
d. 25th September 1984
Character:
Mr. Gruffydd

Maureen O'Hara
b. 17th August 1920
d. 24th October 2015
Character:
Angharad Morgan

Donald Crisp
b. 27th July 1882
d. 25th May 1974
Character:
Gwilym Morgan

Trivia

Interesting Facts

For this film John Ford received his third Academy Award for Best Director, having previously won for The Informer (1935) and The Grapes of Wrath (1940). Eleven years later he would win his fourth for The Quiet Man (1952) (which also starred Maureen O'Hara), a record unmatched by any other director.

It took $110,000 and 150 builders six months to construct Richard Day's elaborate set design on an 80-acre plot in Brent's Crags, near Malibu. The studio brought in blocks of coal weighing over a ton apiece for the construction of the mines and, to create the impression that coal slag covered the landscape in the opening and closing scenes, John Ford had the hillside painted black.

Roddy McDowall had only been in America for two weeks before being cast in the role of Huw. He had been evacuated from Great Britain with his mother and sister to avoid Nazi wartime bombardments.

Although Alfred Newman's justifiably highly-praised score utilised many Welsh melodies as well as the services of virtually every Welsh singer then living in Southern California, his principle love theme was based on the traditional Irish folk song "The Sixpence".

Maureen O'Hara, who was 19 years old at the time of filming, was the film's last surviving cast member at the time of her death (aged 95) in 2015.

Quote

Huw Morgan: *[narrating]* Memory... Strange that the mind will forget so much of what only this moment has passed, and yet hold clear and bright the memory of what happened years ago; of men and women long since dead.

SERGEANT YORK

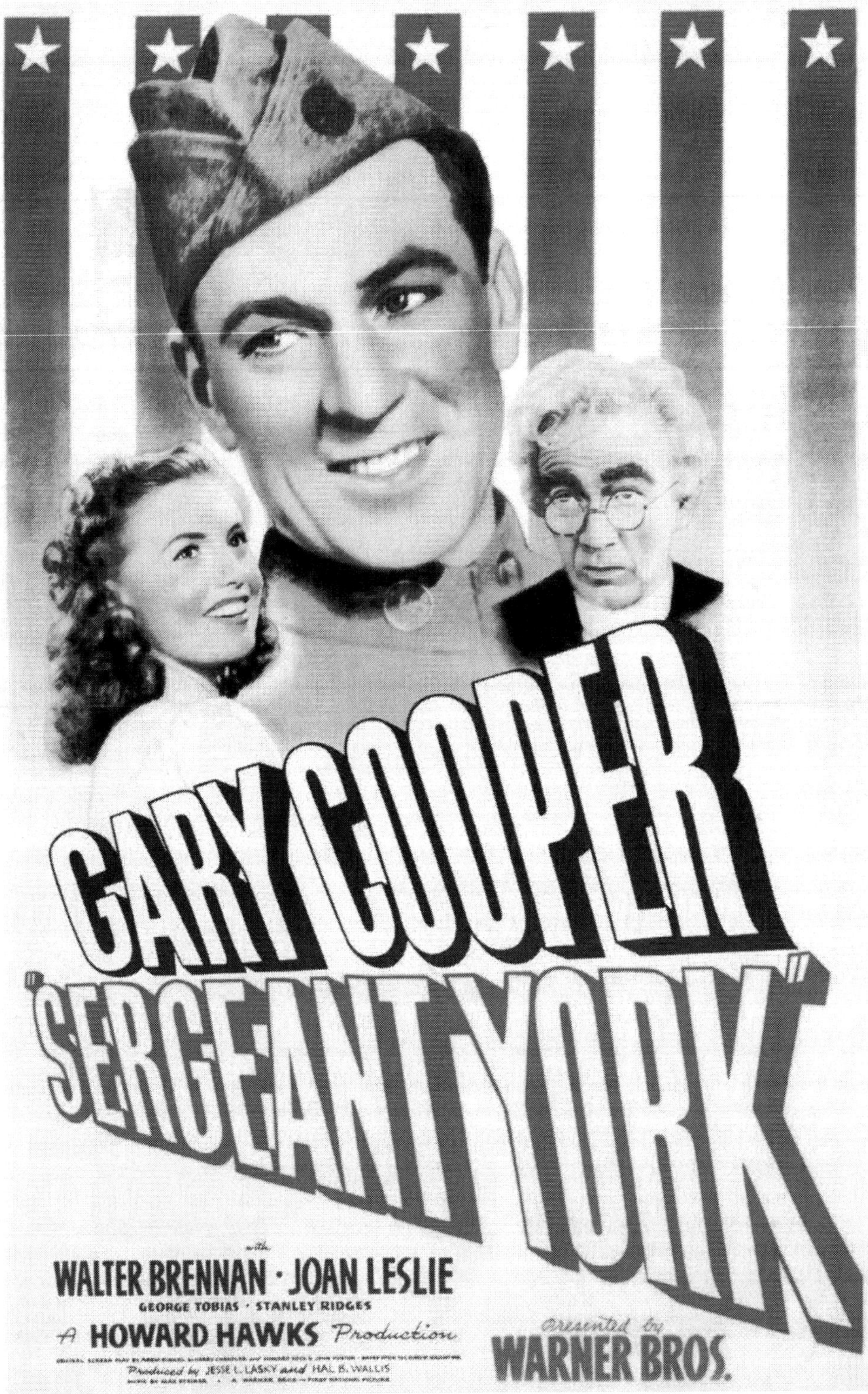

Directed by: Howard Hawks - Runtime: 2h 14min

A marksman is drafted in World War I and ends up becoming one of the most celebrated war heroes.

Starring

Gary Cooper
b. 7th May 1901
d. 13th May 1961
Character:
Alvin C. York

Walter Brennan
b. 25th July 1894
d. 21st September 1974
Character:
Pastor Rosier Pile

Joan Leslie
b. 26th January 1925
d. 12th October 2015
Character:
Gracie Williams

Trivia

Interesting Facts

When informed that Hollywood wanted to make a film about his exploits in World War I, Alvin C. York insisted that only Gary Cooper could play him. At almost 40 years of age Cooper was actually too old to play York - who was not quite 30 at the time of the battle - and York was informed of this, but he insisted that if Cooper couldn't play him, he would not allow the film to be made.

Sergeant York was first film to earn at least 10 Academy Award nominations and not win Best Picture; it won two Academy Awards, Best Actor - Gary Cooper, and Best Film Editing - William Holmes.

In 2008, Sergeant York was selected for preservation in the United States National Film Registry by the Library of Congress as being "culturally, historically, or aesthetically significant".

Alvin C. York himself was on the set for a few days during filming. When one of the crew members tactlessly asked him how many "Jerries" he had killed, York started sobbing so vehemently he threw up. The crew member was nearly fired but the next day York demanded that he keep his job.

This film earned legendary director Howard Hawks his only Best Director Oscar nomination.

Quote

'Pusher' Ross: An' you haven't even seen a subway?
Alvin: I ain't never even heerd o' one.
'Pusher' Ross: 'Heerd'? 'heerd' What kind o' talk is that? Do they all talk that kind of English where you come from?
Alvin: Well there ain't any English people down our way - just Americans.

THE MALTESE FALCON

Directed by: John Huston - Runtime: 1h 40min

San Francisco private eye Sam Spade takes on a case that involves him with three unscrupulous adventurers and their quest for a jewel-encrusted statuette.

Starring

Humphrey Bogart
b. 25th December 1899
d. 14th January 1957
Character:
Samuel Spade

Mary Astor
b. 3rd May 1906
d. 25th September 1987
Character:
Brigid O'Shaughnessy

Gladys George
b. 13th September 1904
d. 8th December 1954
Character:
Iva Archer

Trivia

Goof

[at around 1h 6min] "L.A.F.D." (Los Angeles Fire Department) appears on the firefighters' helmets, the film is set in San Francisco.

Interesting Facts

Warner Bros. planned to change the name of the film to "The Gent from Frisco" because the novel's title had already been used for The Maltese Falcon (1931). The studio eventually agreed to keep the original title at John Huston's insistence.

Although he story-boarded every scene, John Huston was open to abandoning his plans if his more experienced cast came up with something better. He estimated that three-quarters of the time he used his original set-ups, but for the remaining quarter he adopted ideas that the cast had come up with.

Humphrey Bogart had to supply his own wardrobe for the film. This was common practice at Warner Brothers as a way for the studio to save money.

Steve Wynn, the Las Vegas hotel and casino billionaire, paid $4.1 million at auction in 2013 for a statuette of the Maltese Falcon from the film. This makes it one of the most valuable film props ever made, costing more than ten times the films original budget.

Quote

Brigid O'Shaughnessy: Mr. Archer was so alive yesterday, so solid and hearty...
Sam Spade: Stop it. He knew what he was doing. Those are the chances we take.
Brigid O'Shaughnessy: Was he married?
Sam Spade: Yeah, with ten thousand insurance, no children, and a wife that didn't like him.

THE LITTLE FOXES

Directed by: William Wyler - Runtime: 1h 56min

The ruthless moneyed Hubbard clan lives in, and poisons, their part of the deep South at the turn of the twentieth century.

Starring

Bette Davis
b. 5th April 1908
d. 6th October 1989
Character:
Regina Giddens

Herbert Marshall
b. 23rd May 1890
d. 22nd January 1966
Character:
Horace Giddens

Teresa Wright
b. 27th October 1918
d. 6th March 2005
Character:
Alexandra Giddens

Trivia

Interesting Facts

When the film opened at Radio City Music Hall in New York it set an all-time attendance record for a normal opening day with over 22,000 people attending.

According to Samuel Goldwyn Jr., the reason Jack L. Warner loaned Bette Davis to RKO for this film was to settle a $300,000 gambling debt Warner had with Samuel Goldwyn.

Bette Davis had legendary make-up artist Perc Westmore devise a white mask-like effect for her face to emphasise Regina's coldness. Director William Wyler hated it, likening it to a Kabuki mask.

David Hewitt, the character played by Richard Carlson, does not appear at all in the play. He was added to provide a love interest for Alexandra Giddens (Teresa Wright), and to add another sympathetic male character to the film besides Horace Giddens (Herbert Marshall).

The film features Patricia Collinge's (Birdie Hubbard) only Oscar nominated performance.

Quotes

David Hewitt: You know, that's the first time I ever heard your mother tell you to do something, and you didn't hop to do it.
Alexandra Giddens: That's a funny thing to say.
David Hewitt: You know, you take one step. And then you take another. After a while you'll find out you're walking all by yourself.

David Hewitt: Do you like me?
Alexandra Giddens: Not today.
David Hewitt: Why, I'll come back tomorrow.

CITIZEN KANE

Directed by: Orson Welles - Runtime: 1h 59min

Following the death of publishing tycoon Charles Foster Kane, reporters scramble to uncover the meaning of his final word, "Rosebud".

Starring

Orson Welles
b. 6th May 1915
d. 10th October 1985
Character:
Charles Foster Kane

Joseph Cotten
b. 15th May 1905
d. 6th February 1994
Character:
Jedediah Leland

Dorothy Comingore
b. 24th August 1913
d. 30th December 1971
Character:
Susan Alexander Kane

Trivia

Goof

When Susan Alexander Kane tells Kane that she's leaving him once and for all Kane has a moustache. A second later as he watches her walk away the moustache is gone.

Interesting Facts

To keep studio execs off his back, Orson Welles claimed the cast and crew were "in rehearsal" during the first few days of shooting, when in fact they were actually shooting the film. It took a number of days before the studio caught on.

The film's opening - just the title, no star names - was almost unprecedented in 1941. It is now the industry norm for Hollywood blockbusters.

For this film Orson Welles, along with cinematographer Gregg Toland, pioneered "deep focus", a technique that keeps every object in the foreground, centre and background in simultaneous focus. This brought a sense of depth to the two-dimensional world of movies.

Orson Welles' 156-page personal working copy of the script from the film sold for $97,000 in 2007.

Despite all the publicity the film was a box-office flop and was quickly consigned to the RKO vaults. At 1941's Academy Awards it was booed every time one of its nine nominations were announced. In 1998 The American Film Institute's poll ranked the film No.1 on its list of greatest American movies of all time, and No.1 again on its 10th anniversary in 2007.

Quote

Charles Foster Kane: Hello, Jedediah.
Jedediah Leland: Hello, Charlie. I didn't know we were speaking...
Charles Foster Kane: Sure, we're speaking, Jedediah: you're fired.

Sporting Winners

Football

Between 1939 and 1946 normal competitive football was suspended in England and Scotland. Many footballers signed up to fight in the war and as a result many teams were depleted and fielded guest players instead. Appearances in these tournaments did not count in players' official records.

England: The 1940-1941 season was the second season of special wartime football in England. League competition was split into two regional leagues, one North and one South. Teams played as many fixtures as was feasible and winners were decided on goal average rather than points.

Competition	Winner
North Regional League	**Preston North End**
South Regional League	**Crystal Palace**
Football League War Cup	**Preston North End**
London War Cup	**Reading**
Lancashire War Cup	**Manchester United**

Scotland: The 1940-1941 season was the second season of special wartime football in Scotland. The Scottish Football League and Scottish Cup were suspended and in their place regional league competitions were set up.

Competition	Winner
Southern League	**Rangers**
Glasgow Cup	**Celtic**
Southern League Cup	**Rangers**
Summer Cup	**Hibernian**
Renfrewshire Cup	**St Mirren**

International matches: Six unofficial international football games were played in 1941 between England, Scotland and Wales. During this period no caps were awarded.

8/2/1941	England 2-3 Scotland	7/6/1941	Wales 2-3 England
26/4/1941	England 4-1 Wales	4/10/1941	England 2-0 Scotland
3/5/1941	Scotland 1-3 England	25/10/1941	England 2-1 Wales

Rugby - Home Nations

The 1941 Home Nations Championship series was not contested due to the war. International rugby was put on hold and would not resume again until 1947, when the Home Nations would become the Five Nations with the addition of France to the line-up.

Grand National

Although the Grand National was run as normal in 1940 and most other major horse races around the world were able to be held throughout the war, the commandeering of Aintree for defence use in 1941 meant no Grand National could be held between 1941 and 1945.

Epsom Derby - Owen Tudor

The 1941 'New Derby' two furlongs from home; the winner Owen Tudor is far on the right.

Winner.	Jockey	Trainer	Owner	Time
Owen Tudor	**Billy Nevett**	**Fred Darling**	**C. Macdonald-Buchanan**	**2m 32s**

The Derby Stakes is Britain's richest horse race and the most prestigious of the country's five Classics. First run in 1780 this Group 1 flat horse race is open to three year old thoroughbred colts and fillies. Although the race usually takes place at Epsom Downs in Surrey, during both World Wars the venue was changed and the Derby was run at Newmarket; these races are known as the New Derby. *Note: Epsom Downs racecourse was used throughout the war for an anti-aircraft battery.*

Golf - Open Championship

The Open Championship was cancelled in 1941 due to the war and the tournament was not contested again until 1946.

Tennis - Wimbledon

The 1941 Wimbledon Championships was another sporting event cancelled due to World War 2. Hosted since 1877 by the All England Lawn Tennis and Croquet Club in Wimbledon, London, the competition did resume again until 1946.

County Cricket

All first-class cricket was cancelled during the Second World War; no first-class matches were played in England after Friday, 1st September 1939 until Saturday, 19th May 1945.

World Snooker Championship

The World Snooker Championship was cancelled because of the war and was not be held again until 1946.

THE COST OF LIVING

SAVE

FOR NATIONAL SAFETY

DEPOSITS IN TRUSTEE SAVINGS BANKS

help to pay for the cost of the war

ORDINARY ACCOUNTS 2½% per annum

INVESTMENT ACCOUNTS 2¾% per annum

COMPOUND INTEREST

allowed without deductions.
Under direct Government Supervision and control.

YOUR TRUSTEE SAVINGS BANK

COMPARISON CHART

	1941	1941 (+ Inflation)	2020	% Change
3 Bedroom House	£800	£45,084	£234,853	+420.9%
Weekly Income	£2.17s.10d	£162.96	£619	+279.8%
Pint Of Beer	9d	£2.11	£3.79	+79.6%
Cheese (lb)	1s.6d	£4.23	£2.98	-29.6%
Bacon (lb)	1s.10d	£5.17	£2.94	-43.1%
The Beano	2d	47p	£2.75	+485.1%

Shopping

Brooke Bond Beef Cubes (each)	1d
Rowntree's Cocoa (¼lb)	5d
Bournville Cocoa (¼lb)	5d
Cadbury's Bourn-Vita (½lb)	1s.5d
Plain York Chocolate (¼lb block)	4d
Bassett's Liquorice Allsorts (½lb carton)	10d
Amami Wave Sets	7½d
Eve Shampoo	3d
Lux Toilet Soap (tablet)	4d
Lifebuoy Toilet Soap (tablet)	3d
Gillette Razor Blades (3)	1s.3d
Halex Toothbrush	1s
Kolynos Toothpaste	7½d
Phillips' Dental Magnesia	7½d
Pepsodent Irium Dentifrice	7½d
Milk Of Magnesia Tablets	7d
Rennies (25)	7d
Andrews Liver Salt	10½d
Crookes' Halibut Liver Oil (25 capsules)	2s.6d
Ex-Lax Constipation Relief	2½d
Dr Cassells Nerve Tablets	3s.5d
Beechams Lung Syrup (bottle)	1s.4d
Doans Backache Kidney Pills	1s.5d
Germolene Antiseptic Ointment	7d
Germoplast First Aid Adhesive Plaster (tin)	6d
Cro Pax Corn Caps	9d
Sunlight Washing Flakes	6d
George Bell's Cat Powder (10)	7d
Tibs Cat Tonic (9)	7d

DIEU ET MON DROIT
By Appointment
to H.M. The King
Feel its
TONIC ACTION
PEARS'S
ORIGINAL
TRANSPARENT SOAP
You can actually feel Pears Soap doing your skin good while you are washing. A pleasant tingling sensation tells you that its special tonic properties are reviving the vitality which is the secret of a healthy complexion. Pears Soap wears down without waste to the thinnest wafer, and is the most economical of all good toilet soaps.
Pears
TRANSPARENT SOAP
6D. A CAKE
MATCHLESS FOR THE COMPLEXION
TP 238/19

CLOTHES

Women's Clothing

Samuel Soden Marmot Wallaby Fur Coat	23gns
J. A. Davis & Co Woollen Coat	£5.5s
Schofields Spring Felt Hat	19s.3d
C&A Junior Miss Dress (5 coupons)	19s.11d
Barkers Utility Stockings	2s
Suedette Perforated Court Shoe	8s.11d
Glace Court Slippers	5s.11d

Men's Clothing

Austin Reed Great Coat	10gns
Man's Finest Cloth Suit	5gns
Wilson Brothers Busmen's Suit	£1.12s.6d
Army Boots	10s.6d

The best
HOME DEFENCE
against
dull cooking
is
BOVRIL
Bovril stimulates the digestive process on which vitality and health depend. It enables you to get full benefit from your food. Bovril makes meals much nicer, as well as more nourishing.

GRANT'S
Scotch
WHISKY
Aged · Of Rare Mellowness ·
Subtle Bouquet ·
BY HOST · BY GUEST ·
BY ALL PREFERRED!

Smoke
GREYS
CIGARETTES
Just honest-to-goodness pre-war tobacco
10 FOR 9D
Plain (Green Label) or Cork-tipped (Red Label)

BEER IS BEST!
AT ALL ROYAL BREWERY HOUSES
Fight Winter Chills With
BURTON
An Excellent Beer
BEER IS BEST
SUPPORT YOUR LOCAL RED CROSS FUND

FOR EMERGENCY SANITATION
SAN IZAL
6D
SANIZAL

Other Prices

HMV 10in Record	2s.5½d
Suit Dry Cleaning & Tailor Pressing	1s.9d
Osbaldiston's Ladies Shopping Bag	3s.6d
Gents Hide Leather Dressing Case	25s
Ladies Brush Set	10s.6d
Lewis's Ready Mixed Paint (5lb tin)	2s
Nutilis Vegetable Fertilizer (bag)	6d
Gumption Smooth Paste Cleaner	6d
White Grape Australian Wine	5s.6d
King Six Cigar (each)	8d
Player's Digger Flake Tobacco (1oz)	1s.3½d
Capstan Navy Cut Cigarettes (20)	1s.5½d
Woman's Weekly Magazine	3d

TOP PRICE

FOR YOUR

OLD GOLD or SILVER

38/- GIVEN FOR YOUR SOVEREIGNS

BLACKWOOD'S, 43, BRIGGATE, SHIPLEY.

Money Conversion Table

Pounds / Shillings / Pence 'Old Money'		Decimal Value	Value 2020 (Rounded)
Farthing	¼d	0.1p	6p
Half Penny	½d	0.21p	12p
Penny	1d	0.42p	23p
Threepence	3d	1.25p	70p
Sixpence	6d	2.5p	£1.41
Shilling	1s	5p	£2.82
Florin	2s	10p	£5.64
Half Crown	2s.6d	12.5p	£7.04
Crown	5s	25p	£14.09
Ten Shillings	10s	50p	£28.18
Pound	20s	£1	£56.36
Guinea	21s	£1.05	£59.17
Five Pounds	£5	£5	£281.78
Ten Pounds	£10	£10	£563.55

SMEDLEY'S

ENGLISH GROWN

Garden Peas

7d, 8½d and 1/1 per tin

ROBINSON'S (DRIFFIELD) LTD.

Family Grocers and Provision Merchants

Tea Blenders and Coffee Specialists

53 Market Place, Driffield. Phone 37.

DIAMOND
ENGAGEMENT RINGS
£5, £10 to £100.
WATCHES
WATCH REPAIRS.

JOHN
DYSON
& SONS
24-26, BRIGGATE
LEEDS

We are Buyers of
OLD GOLD
SECOND-HAND
JEWELLERY and
DIAMONDS

THE BATTLE OF THE ATLANTIC

SPADE versus SUBMARINE

WANTED BY EASTER

150 New Allotment Tenants

FOR

150 New Allotments

NOW READY AND WAITING

AT

RED BECK (near Norwood Terrace)
WROSE
NAB WOOD DRIVE
SPRINGSWOOD
MANOR LANE
WEST ROYD (Leeds Road)

RENT FREE THIS YEAR

Tenancy Guaranteed until End of War.

Apply personally, or by letter or postcard :—

TOWN HALL, SHIPLEY (Clerk's Department)

or any member Shipley Home Food Production Corps.

VEGETABLES — VITAMINS — VICTORY

CARTOONS

The New Order changeth, giving place to Newer.

"Blimey! That's what I told him, sir! But he said 'Rubbish! a man's as old as he feels'!"

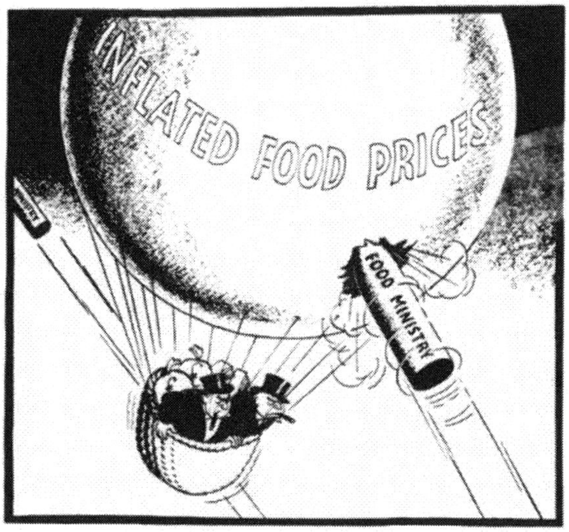

Coming Down!

"THAT'S NOT HISTORY, MUSSO—THAT'S US!"

Printed in Great Britain
by Amazon

66195305R00036

13th Age

Game Master's Screen and Resource Book

A *13th Age* Supplement

by Cal Moore and Wade Rockett

Pelgrane Press

13th Age is a fantasy roleplaying game by
Rob Heinsoo, Jonathan Tweet, Lee Moyer, & Aaron McConnell

Fire Opal

www.fireopalmedia.com and **www.pelgranepress.com**

CREDITS

Publishers
Simon Rogers, Cathriona Tobin

Designers
Cal Moore, Wade Rockett

Editing & Development
Rob Heinsoo

Screen Artists
Lee Moyer, Aaron McConnell

Interior Art
Aaron McConnell, Rich Longmore, and Lee Moyer

Layout
Chris Huth

Special Thanks

Thanks to Jon Spengler of Dorkadia for suggestions on how the players can drive the stories, Martin Killman and Ryven Cedrylle for making every icon roll count, Philippe-Antoine Menard for a great strategy for crafting backgrounds, and Sean Swanwick for wise words on backgrounds.

TABLE OF CONTENTS

Introduction

"We have targeted the game toward experienced gamemasters and players at all levels of roleplaying experience."

That's the very first line of rules text in the *13th Age* core book, and it's there for an important reason. The game was envisioned as an opportunity for Rob Heinsoo and Jonathan Tweet to share with other GMs how they run d20-rolling fantasy roleplaying games with their own friends. It's based on their hacks, house rules, GM styles, and personal philosophies about how such games can be designed and run so they offer everyone involved the most opportunities for fun. As a result of this approach, *13th Age* sometimes demands more improvisation and rules adjudication from GMs than games which are designed for GMs who are complete beginners.

We like to support our GMs by answering questions and supplying them with resources and guidance, and have long felt that a completely GM-focused product would be a great addition to the *13th Age* line. We hope the tools included with the *Game Master's Screen and Resource Book* serve you well.

Our goal for the screen is to provide useful tables, charts, and reminders to keep your game running smoothly by providing the information you need, without having to open a book. For this *Resource Book*, we want to offer GMs ideas to help them run better games, and make it easier to handle the improvisational parts. We cover subjects that generate a lot of questions on forums, at conference panels, and even in our own games. Where it makes sense, we've also incorporated existing material into the guide that is useful to any GM, such as montages from the organized play program, along with a simple index of valuable advice from the rest of the "core" sources.

The guide starts with Rob and Jonathan's **advice to *13th Age* designers**, adapted for GMs, and covers their goals for the system.

The **adventure toolkit** provides a step-by-step process designed to help GMs who need to run a quick adventure on the fly, such as a demo or convention pick-up game.

The **montage system**, which ASH Law uses in the organized play adventures, provides GMs with a player-driven method of creating action in between encounters and battles.

Next, we dig into **how to best use the icon relationship dice**, a core idea of the *13th Age* rules. The advice covers a range of ideas and examples for incorporating those 5s and 6s.

As with any F20 system, battles are a key component to *13th Age* play, and we discuss strategies for building fun, balanced (or not), and **exciting battles** for your game.

Although *13th Age* is a gridless system that uses streamlined rules for combat, **incorporating terrain** into your battles can make your fights more dynamic and fun. This section provides ideas on how to do that.

Backgrounds are one of the game's more free-form mechanics, and can require some negotiation between players and GMs. We go into the key components of what makes a good background and why those stories are important, as well as how to adjust for generalists who might try to take advantage of the system.

For players, the GM's world usually truly comes to life through the NPCs they interact with. In this section, we offer advice on how to **make your NPCs more interesting**, and provide you with some icon-related NPCs that you can easily insert into your adventures.

A GM guide wouldn't be complete without a section from Rob or Jonathan, and here Rob provides **some new ideas** that they've had since the release of the core book. We're sure you'll find something fun to try.

Finally, we included an **index of valuable advice** sections from a range of sources for easy reference. We also included a template sheet for GMs to track PC and icon relationships.

Whether you use only a few of these ideas or many, we hope they make it easier for you to run your games and make those games more fun for both you and your players. Game on!

DESIGN AESTHETIC

Designing material for *13th Age* is subtly different than designing material for other F20 roleplaying games. These notes are based on the guidelines that Rob gives to designers working on *13th Age* products. Because advice for creators of *13th Age* books can be helpful to creators of homebrew *13th Age* material, we've included it here along with advice on how GMs can apply certain guidelines to their own games.

What Is This F20 You Speak Of?

Instead of repeating "d20-rolling fantasy game" over and over, we sometimes use "F20" to refer to a category which includes the World's Most Popular Role Playing Game as well as other d20-rolling fantasy games that must respond in one way or another to the assumptions Gary Gygax and Dave Arneson rolled out nearly four decades ago—but not those d20-rolling games that dispense with the halberds and dungeon-bashing model. As with so many other things, we owe a debt of gratitude to Robin D. Laws for coming up with this term and its elegantly-worded definition.

Writers: We Are Not Telling the Story!

The biggest difference between most 13th Age *writing and that of other RPGs and worlds is that* 13th Age *support material never tells the full story. The goal of* 13th Age *design is to spur individual players and GMs to create their own exciting ideas.*

We often receive first drafts of 13th Age *content about specific locations and organizations that begin with a short story about how that location started and developed into its current state; or specific, canonical details on how that organization operates. We revise most of these first drafts because the goal of* 13th Age *design isn't to detail only one way that GMs and players should bring a new element into their campaigns: it's to provide them with exciting ideas they might not have come up with themselves, and offer hooks they can experiment with in many different styles of campaign.*

Instead of telling a single story and filling in the details, we aim to make GMs and players feel excited about having tweaked or improved ideas to make them their own. What might seem like incomplete design in other games or game worlds is the product of deliberate exclusion in 13th Age *design. That's where GMs and players come in; they're the ones who will take a hook or possible story thread and turn it into a memorable character or campaign.*

Of course, it's lame to truly just leave things incomplete and say, "Hey, it's up to you and you are limited only by your imagination!" So our standard approach is to make it clear that there isn't just one possible story. There's a multitude of ways different campaigns could use the material we're presenting, and we try to acknowledge some of those possibilities from the start. By mentioning some exciting possibilities, we give people who are going to use our suggestions the agency of choosing options that work best for them, while providing examples to the GMs and players who prefer being inspired to come up with their own riffs.

Here are some examples of how we generally want to approach design. In each section, we apply that same design intent to GM advice on how to handle a home campaign.

Half-orcs in the Empire: *A lot of games would be comfortable with text saying that such and such an Emperor signed a treaty with a particular half-orc chieftain and that this helped give half-orcs official status in the Dragon Empire.* 13th Age *says that an earlier Emperor recognized half-orcs as full citizens, but it leaves all the details open. If we had named the Emperor, or the battles, we would have been whittling down the things that players can invent as part of their backgrounds and One Unique Thing.*

GMs: As a GM, you can create a specific story about half-orcs (or whatever) for your campaign. But if you want to apply the game's design approach at your table, try leaving room for the players to change those details, or add their own. That way, you and the players create those elements together, dividing up the job of world building and sharing the story.

Nagas: *When the* 13th Age Bestiary *introduced a version of nagas, it included a fairly long discussion of possible naga histories. It was not "the" history of nagas. There were options for between five and seven interpretations of what was going on with the race, all of which fit with the same curious game mechanics in which nagas reflect or absorb magic and grow smaller as they grow older.*

GMs: Sometimes you want to use the adventure or campaign to create a particular story arc involving a monster, icon, location, or organization. But in general we recommend building in options for several possible truths, leaving the final interpretation to the players. This doesn't necessarily mean that you come right out and tell the players, "You guys get to decide what's going on here." Instead, you can start with a range of possibilities, then decide what's true in your game based on the PCs' backgrounds and One Unique Things, and the ideas the players throw around at the table. Don't telegraph that you're listening so closely to them: sometimes the best ideas are the things they express as ridiculous fears! ("What if the Priestess has secretly been trying to kill us all along?") For more on that, see Rob's "Chum the Adventure" options on the screen.

Horizon in 13 True Ways: *There are many useful details about Horizon in the write-up. But there are huge question marks, including a sidebar on different ways you could interpret the awesome art that shows the floating city and its great port below, and each interpretation might result in a very different campaign.*

GMs: Perhaps you know exactly how you want to portray a location in the campaign, such as a major city. But be open to making changes based on player input, so that it better supports the story the players want to tell at the table with their characters. You don't always have to completely change things either, but offer an option for a character willing to look for it. Maybe Horizon is the city of magic, but it also has a famous witch-hunter school in one section of the city that trains fighters to combat those who use dark magic. That wasn't the plan for Horizon to start, but it helps one of the PCs fit into Horizon as their "home town."

Blood & Lightning: *As a minor example, consider the sample adventure in the* 13th Age *core rulebook. Since we want to encourage each table to play with icons and motives that matter to the PCs at the table, there are three versions of who might control Boltstrike Pillar. Similarly, the very first encounter is a battle with goblins, and there are three different suggested variations on the goblins depending on which enemy icon is best for your group's storyline.*

GMs: This idea of pitting enemies relevant to the PCs' icons against the party runs through most every *13th Age* adventure. Reflavoring a group of tribal orc sentries in service to the Orc Lord as a band of skullface-painted crypt guardians in service to the Lich King only requires a bit of description, and results in a battle that's significant to the PCs who have that icon relationship.

Not One Story, But Many Possible Stories

If you're designing for others and you find yourself writing details that feel like they came from a specific campaign, you're going to want to phrase those details as possibilities, while keeping your writer's eye open for the subtle ways that different stories would open up in other campaigns.

GMs: If you're writing for your own home campaign, think about the outcomes you want to achieve, but give your players some possibilities for that outcome, and see which ones they might latch onto.

For example, as a designer, you aren't telling just your story of a magical location and a dangerous organization that inhabits the place. You're creating a tool that will inspire many different game groups to create their own compelling and unpredictable stories. There's almost always room for elements of the story-you-really-want-to-tell, but that singular story is not the point, and if it looks like your design only has one point, or one useful approach, odds are we'll challenge you to revise it for broader application.

GMs: You know the story of the magical location, and you have a backstory in mind about how it's an old bastion from the Wizard King's time, which plays to a *unique* of one of the PCs. But maybe instead you layer in clues and rumors which open up a few options for that location: Maybe the group running the place is some off-branch of the Elf Queen's dark elf sorcerers, or a disavowed mage once high in the Archmage's service. Most of the details of the place can be the same, but see which entry point gets the players the most excited and go from there.

13th Age Monster Design

Monster design is a huge topic, but here are a few key issues that keep coming up. GMs, this advice applies to you the same as designers.

While it's true that not all monsters need to be innovative, the single most common mistake you'll see in monster design for 13th Age *is design that fails to add anything to the experience at the table that's not already present in many other monsters. If you find yourself designing a monster that does nothing but daze or hamper foes, or maybe does a bit more damage with a high dice roll, realize that you're creating a very generic monster that functions pretty much like most other monsters.*

That may not be a bad thing. That may be exactly what you want. (In which case you may ask yourself why you need a new monster at all; perhaps you should be using something that's already published. . . .) But you probably have some interesting backstory for that monster, so why not give it mechanics that fit your interesting story?

Our starting point for monster design is usually to think about the psychology of the experience, asking how we want players to feel as they're fighting the monster. Should it creep them out? Make them laugh? Scare the crap out of them? Freak them out as it does something unexpected? With that as a starting point, you can design mechanics to fit that story to get the feel you're going for.

Another issue that comes up is mechanics that aren't fun. Sure, you might design a set of monster abilities that are interesting to you, but in play, does it slow combat down and just bring up a lot of questions from the players on how "so-and-so" works? Best to look for a simpler option; there's probably something that has a similar effect or that's already been published as part of another monster that will work just as well. If not, then go ahead and create it, but always keep in mind how much fun it will be for the players to face, and not only how much fun it might be for you to run.

GMs: It's fun when our monsters do things that surprise us as much as they do the players, using mechanics that are built-in. And when the game stays fun for us, we want to run more often, and that keeps everyone happy.

But there's a corollary that's easy to lose track of, which applies to your experience at the table. If there's a monster that you and your players don't find fun when it hits the table, either because it slows things down or seems stupid or just leads to dumb stories, you don't have to use it as written.

One option to spice up an un-fun monster during a battle is to change an ability on the fly. It's simple to swap in abilities from other monsters—if the players aren't enjoying their fight with an owlbear, imagine their surprise when its feathers suddenly glow orange and it breathes a gout of flame onto the paladin. If you're making up a brand-new ability on the spot and you're not sure what its impact is going to be, make it a limited-use ability (once per battle is always safe). It's big and scary and has an impact, but it's not happening again . . . at least, not until the escalation die is 5 or 6 maybe. You could tell the PCs they need to finish things off fast because it looks like your monster is going to do THAT again.

13th Age Adventure Toolkit

What Is an Adventure Toolkit?

Sometimes a GM is asked to run a *13th Age* game with little or no preparation. Icon relationships, backgrounds, and One Unique Things provide a great foundation for an improvised adventure, giving the GM a way to draw out story hooks from the players. But if you aren't comfortable with a lot of improvising (or you're just feeling brain-dead at the moment), a pre-made structure can help you turn those hooks into a satisfying and fun adventure.

That's where the Adventure Toolkit comes in. It provides a basic framework for an adventure, and distributes the task of improvisational adventure-building storytelling around the table.

Building Your Adventure

Here's how to create an improvised *13th Age* adventure using this toolkit:

1: **Decide what the adventure will be about:** Have your players choose two *themes* from the list provided, or create their own.

2: **Decide what will happen during the adventure:** Using the *adventure plot template*, work with your players to create a plotline that will bring those themes to life.

3: **Run the resulting adventure:** Use the simple *framework* we provide, which consists of a montage, skill challenges, and battles. Plan for two scenes focused on skill challenges and two battles per two-hour session.

Step One: Choose Two Themes

As the first building block to create adventures, we're borrowing the concept of themes from Robin D. Laws' excellent RPG *Hillfolk*.

A *theme* is a broad, simple, abstract concept that evokes some aspect of the human condition. Your plot will describe what happens in the adventure; themes describe what the adventure is about.

For example, an adventure in which the PCs get involved with a feud between two barbarian tribes could be about Ancestral Sins, Blood Ties, Change Is Hard, Choosing Sides, Loyalty, New Beginnings, Old Memories, Reckonings, Two Wrongs Don't Make a Right, or Vengeance.

If you like, you can get this started by choosing one theme yourself and turning the other over to the players. It also works to choose one theme and wait for others to emerge during play. Or you could offer hints while letting all themes emerge during the game.

Have Your Players Choose Two Themes from This List:

Ambition
Ancestral Sins
Betrayal
Blood Ties
Buzzards Circle
Cages
Change Is Hard
Charity
Choosing Sides
Condemned to Freedom
Creation
Destruction
Divinity
Dying Well
False Smiles
Fear
Fear of the Unknown
Forgiveness
Gold
Guilt
Heartache
Heating Up
Home
Justice
Knowing Too Much
Lion's Den
Losing
Losing Control
Loyalty
Masks
The Morning After
New Beginnings
Old Memories
Outsiders
Predator and Prey
Preservation
Progress
Rebirth
Reckonings
Redemption
Ritual
Secrets
Small Details
Thresholds
Ties that Bind
Truth
Trust
Two Wrongs Don't Make a Right
Unity
Vengeance
What Price Victory?

Step Two: Generate a Plot

Read the following sentence aloud to the players:

"In this adventure, the characters must [ACTION] [OBJECT] in order to [GOAL] for [ICON]. But [COMPLICATION]!"

This is your *adventure plot template*. Ask the players to fill in the blanks with an action, an object the characters act on, a goal, and a complication.

Here are some general ideas—but the more specific your group can get, the better:

Sample actions: Guard, recover, save, destroy, help, foil, plunder, find, hide, kill, heal, journey to, escape from, summon, banish, exorcise, overthrow, restore, explore, identify, smuggle, protect, kidnap, defend, solve, claim.

Sample objects: Monster, magic item, large sum of money, valuable object, royalty/aristocrat, wealthy merchant, struggling merchant, caravan, treasure ship, prison, prison ship, flying prison, vault, husband/wife/daughter/son, temple, sacred spot, castle, keep, city, village, tribe, tomb, pass, river, mountain, true heir, pretender, ancient secret, political intrigue, mystery.

Sample goals: Get paid, bring peace, defeat evil, achieve justice, liberate the oppressed, protect the innocent, unify that which is divided, heal old wounds, fulfill a debt, placate a supernatural being, settle a disagreement, reveal a hidden truth.

Sample complications: The hunter becomes the hunted, the true enemy reveals itself, the true mission is deadlier than they imagined, the price of victory might be too high, they might be on the wrong side, getting there won't be easy, a different icon has other plans.

Step Three: Run the Adventure

A roleplaying game adventure consists of several connected scenes in which the players try to achieve a practical, external goal using their characters' powers and their own wits. Because you're making this adventure up on the spot, we're going to keep the structure simple and linear:

Scene 1: Montage
Scene 2: First Challenge
Scene 3: First Battle
Scene 4: Second Challenge
Scene 5: Second (Final) Battle, and Resolution

Using the completed adventure plot template as a guide, decide where the adventure begins: a remote fishing village, the outskirts of an orc-infested forest, the foothills of a haunted mountain, the right eye socket of a dead god's massive skull, or another suitable starting point.

Scene 1: Montage

Movies about fantasy heroics don't linger on every battle fought, and every obstacle overcome. Instead, they use a montage of scenes that tell the story of all sorts of exciting things that happened on the way to the real adventure, and that the heroes emerged victorious from each encounter. Use montages to kick off the session.

Tell the players that their characters just undertook a long and difficult journey to get to the spot where the adventure begins.

Turn to the player on your left and ask them to describe one threat or obstacle that the party faced on their journey toward the location where the adventure begins. The obstacle could be large (a dangerous ambush, or an avalanche) or small (someone stole the cleric's trousers).

Turn to the next player clockwise and tell them that their character did something impressive to overcome that threat or obstacle. Ask them to describe what they did. Don't make them roll dice at this point—this event happened in the past, and they succeeded.

Continue around the group until every player has had a chance to invent an obstacle and describe how their characters overcame an obstacle. If some players aren't comfortable with making something up on the spot, feel free to coach them, or turn their one- or two-word answer into something bigger.

See the next section beginning on page 11 for more discussion of montages along with extended examples.

Scene 2: First Challenge

In this scene, the characters must overcome a major obstacle that stands between them and their goal, using roleplaying, skill checks, or a combination of each.

Offer the players multiple ways to get past the obstacle, each one with its own benefits and potential downsides. Each challenge also requires something different from the PCs in order to succeed:

- Skill checks using different backgrounds, where failure either does damage to the PCs, results in the loss of a useful item, or delays them so their enemies have time to prepare for their arrival.
- Icon relationship checks, either made on the spot or rolled before play began and held in reserve. A 6 with one or more relevant icons gets the party past the obstacle. A 5 also gets the party past the obstacle, but at a cost of HP, recoveries, a minor side quest, or a meaningful limitation such as, "You may pass, as long as you do not shed the blood of a goblin this day." (And of course, there's a battle coming up with goblins in it. . . .)

Scene 3: First Battle

At last, the PCs get to hit someone! Create an opposing force using the Building Battles chart from the GM screen (or on page

203 of the core rulebook), or grab a group of enemies from an existing *13th Age* adventure.

Make this battle challenging, but mostly fair. (The unfair fight comes later, at the end). The enemies should be relevant to the icons in play, and their presence must make sense in the context of the plot you generated in step 2. Also, take into account what happened during the previous scene. Did the kobolds spot the party as they climbed the treacherous cliff, and have they prepared a trap? Did a PC anger a fire elemental, who set the gnoll tribe's tents ablaze as it stomped away?

Scene 4: Second Challenge

If the PCs defeat their first set of enemies, they must now overcome a more difficult—and deadlier—challenge to reach the next battle. Increase the DC of the skill checks, and make the consequences of failure (and the complications arising from an icon relationship roll of 5) more serious.

The first challenge probably involved relatively straightforward actions, such as bargaining with ogres, or steering a ship. This challenge is where things get weird, *13th Age* style. Maybe the PCs have to jump from gear to gear in a huge dwarven machine, enter the subconscious mind of a demon prince, or play soccer against a legion of ghost soldiers. Try to come up with something fun and different.

Scene 5: Second (Final) Battle, and Resolution

There's only one thing that stands between the PCs and their goal now, and it's an enemy that is clearly the villain of the adventure. Whether it's an orc general, a dragonic cult leader who's ascended to demigodhood, an alien monstrosity from beyond space and time, or a rival party who are even meaner and more powerful than the PCs, now is when you unleash a challenge worth telling about.

You can use skill checks to make this fight really interesting—what if the PCs had to fight their way through hordes of skeletal mooks on a rickety bridge while dodging orcish arrows and kobold bombs, knowing that the Empire will fall to the Lich King if they don't reach the Altar of Unlife quickly? Exciting stuff! You can read more about using terrain effectively in battle on page 36.

After the battle ends, the PCs will have resolved the central problem in the adventure—or not.

Either way, the outcome needs to be satisfying. Maybe your players will tell a story about the time they accidentally ended the world, and it was *awesome*.

Once the adventure is resolved, the PCs can go on their way toward the next story, or you can generate one all over again. Have fun!

MONTAGES

The following section embraces and expands upon the montage system that ASH Law uses in the *13th Age* organized play adventures and that we briefly discuss in Scene 1 of the GM Toolkit. Montages are a useful tool that can be incorporated into any *13th Age* game.

Sometimes you don't want to take the time to go into the details of a trip or activity the heroes are undertaking but do want to give a sense of time passing and what's happening to the heroes during that period. Whether it's overland travel, random dungeon exploration, or even fortifying an old farmhouse against zombies, you can use montages to quickly advance the story while co-creating events and interactions that may contribute in surprising ways later in the session or the campaign.

Start with a player who is comfortable improvising and ask them to describe a problem that the party faces as they travel or undertake an activity, without offering a solution. Then turn to the player to the left of the starting player and ask *them* how their PC does something clever or awesome to solve the problem. After they narrate a solution, ask that same player to describe the *next* obstacle that the group must deal with. The next player clockwise gets to solve the new problem, then offer up a new obstacle, and so on around the table until everyone has invented and solved a problem.

Encourage players creating solutions to draw on any aspect of their character or invent something new, but don't call for any die rolls, even when the solution to a challenge involves combat. These events occur in quick narrative time, and allow the players to invent stories to reinforce their characters' defining qualities, whether those details involve icon relationships, *uniques*, or backgrounds. Their stories can also mention the use of powers their PCs might have, but they won't actually use any resources in providing a solution. Pay attention to the vignettes the players create for the montage, because those story elements provide excellent source material you can revisit later in the campaign to strengthen each PC's story. When you do so, it reinforces the idea that you and the players are creating a shared story experience as they see elements they created come into play.

While the players are generating their obstacles and ways to overcome those challenges, you (the GM) still play a part in the montage stories. As each player tells you how their PC solved the problem, narrate back to the group what that PC did, but put a spin on it to highlight the character's heroism, wit, or humor. You don't want to change the core idea they give you too much, but this is your chance to add small details about the PC and the world that help make the story come alive for the players, possibly revealing new information to them or even foreshadowing events to come.

Depending on your group, keep in mind that players will start with different comfort levels with the montage process. Some players will offer so many details and wild ideas that you won't have much to add when you play the scene back with embellishments. Other players will choose to provide the bare minimum. It's okay if you or even the other players offer suggestions to reluctant talkers to help flesh out a problem or solution, but the player should always have final say on what they present. After seeing what other players come up with in a few montages, the process should become smoother for everyone, with more wild, creative, inspirational, and fun outcomes. Once players see something they narrate re-enter the game in some way at a later point, they'll be more likely to offer up stories they care about.

One last note. Not every description is created equal, but each description is valid in its own right. The player who suggests an obstacle of "I lose my left boot and begin tripping everywhere I go" is as valid an option as another player who says "A pack of giant slavers begins tracking the party." As GM, you might suggest that the first PC's tripping problem causes a ruckus with someone they fall into who wants to squash them, to add an element of danger or conflict for the next player to resolve, but let the group decide what's fun for them.

Example I: Shipping to New Port

Here's an example of the montage rules in play. The players have hired a ship in Axis and are traveling to New Port, a trip of up to a week depending on the winds. The GM doesn't have any specific encounters in mind until they reach New Port, so it's time for a montage of the trip by the players. The GM shows the players the Dragon Empire map, to give them an idea of the geography in case anyone needs some inspiration.

Problem (player 1): "Soon after leaving Azure Bay, the ship gets dry docked on the back of a giant sea turtle that breaches. We're stuck, and the turtle is going south not east."

Solution (player 2): "This isn't a problem. My master revealed a secret about turtles to me when I was a girl. The back of their necks are ticklish, and they'll go underwater to make that stop. I tickle the giant turtle and it dives into the sea."

GM embellishment: "In an act of amazing bravery and skill, [player 2's PC] tickles the turtle. As it suddenly descends, she runs like a gazelle across the water-slick shell, leaping to the ship's rigging just before the vortex of sea from the turtle's descent pulls her into the depths."

Problem (player 2): "The next day as the Necropolis comes into sight, a heavy fog rises. There are strange wails around the ship, and then foul, undead spirits begin attacking us."

Solution (player 3): "I've heard stories about dead sailors lost off the coast of the Necropolis. They see those waters as their domain and require payment to pass. I throw a handful of silver into the mist."

GM embellishment: "[Player 3's PC] walks to the side of the ship where the mist-spirits swarm. Courageously, knowing he could be torn to shreds, he holds out a handful of silver, offering words of appeasement before throwing the coins into the mist. The spirits apparently accept the offering, since the attacks stop and the fog shreds away before anyone has been seriously hurt."

Problem (player 3): "As the ship passes the peninsula holding Vigil, the crew discovers the ships' rum supply has gone foul. They immediately threaten to mutiny if the captain doesn't head for Santa Cora to resupply."

Solution (player 4): "As a bard, I dig deep into my best stories, keeping the crew entertained and working hard as they listen to my tales and making the time pass quickly as they forget their grog."

GM embellishment: "Days seem like hours as [player 3's PC] tells roaring tales of adventure and heroism about the heroes of old, including a tale about the centaurs of Wild Wood that is quite rousing. The bard's voice is hoarse and mouth dry by the end, but she is so entertaining that the crew is more productive than they've ever been and you're ahead of schedule."

Problem (player 4): "We're a half day's journey from New Port when a pirate ship is sighted. They drive hard, seeking to take us, and have our crew outnumbered."

Solution (player 1): "Seeing that we can't outrun them and will have to fight, I use a ritual to create illusionary crew members while we hide below. When the pirates board us, they attack the illusions, letting us surprise them."

GM embellishment: "Your time among the crew pays off, and you create great illusions of them manning their stations. When the first wave of pirates boards, they are totally fooled as you and the rest of the crew surge out, quickly overcoming them. As you send them overboard, alive or dead, the pirate ship pulls away, her captain cursing defeat in a language you don't recognize. Yet."

Example 2: Glitterhaegen to Anvil

The second example is also a travel story, but this time the journey is on land. The GM tells the players they are traveling from Glitterhaegen to Anvil through the Bitterwood in the Dragon Empire. Each player must offer a problem and solution, narrating the trip.

Problem (player 1): "As we pass through the forest, a goblin raiding party comes over a wooded rise about half a mile away. There's a lot of the buggers."

Solution (player 2): "Let's give those goblins something else to worry about. There are owlbear tracks in the area. I'll distract the goblins and lead them right to the beast."

GM embellishment: "[Player 2's PC] moves forward and out of sight like the expert tracker she is while the rest of you hide. Soon you hear her scream a few curse words in goblin, followed by a scream of pain from a goblin hit by an arrow and yells and thrashing from the rest of the goblins as they crash after the ranger. Seconds later there's an ear-grating owlbear roar and you see the goblin war party fleeing through the woods pursued by an owlbear with a goblin's arm in its mouth. The ranger soon returns with a smile."

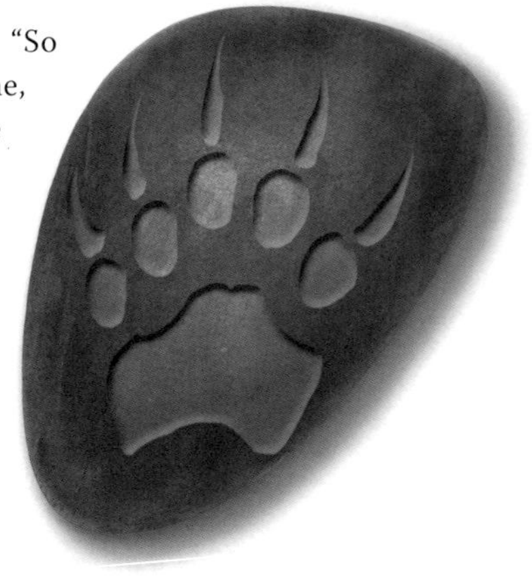

Problem (player 2): "So everything is going fine, but storm clouds come up thick and fast and begin spraying lightning. We can see the storm coming, it's going to hit us here in the trees, and it's going to be nasty.""

Solution (player 3): "I don't know if this is a normal storm or not. And I don't care. Because I've spent enough time on weather duty with my icon, the Archmage, to recognize that there's a storm ward just over the hill to the north. So I get the ranger to lead us quickly over the hill and then I do some wizardly hand-waving to get the storm ward firing at full strength."

GM embellishment: "The ranger gets you over the hill in time and you were right, the plinth holding the storm ward is still strong and shielded. You get the blue flame sparking before the worst of the rain hits and the lightning and thunder roll far past you. You even get a great rainbow."

Problem (player 3): "The storm ward worked. But there were consequences farther on. A river in a wide valley we must pass through on our way to Anvil has overflown its banks, flooding the area and making passage difficult and dangerous. Going around will cost us days of delay."

Solution (player 4): "In my younger days, I was a Razoredge Gorge raft guide. I show the others how to construct a sturdy raft and navigate us safely to the far side of the valley."

GM embellishment: "It's a wild ride, with lots of floating debris and unexpected obstacles. [Player 4's PC] guides you through it all, expertly keeping the raft from flipping and completely avoiding 'something large' moving underwater near one of the holes you were heading for. You arrive on the far side no worse the wear except for being damp."

Problem (player 4): "The raft ride put us off the main path. As we try to find our way back to it, we enter a hollow with a mining camp set up on low ground. Our appearance upsets a family of dwarves mining their claim, and the whole clan doesn't seem to be right in the head as they discuss how they have to kill and eat us now, out loud among themselves."

Solution (player 1): "Um, cannibal dwarves? I don't know. Should we just kill them all? That doesn't sound like what I'd do."

GM: "Right, you're not usually the killer type. So how do you like solving problems?"

Player 1: "Stealing things. I don't know how that's going to work."

GM: "Well, also being tricky, sometimes."

Player 1: "Yeah. Oh. That would work. OK. As the dwarves discuss which one of us to eat first, I listen in and get a few of their names. Then I imitate voices and start making claims and insults to get them fighting with each other while we hightail it out of there."

GM embellishment: "With perfect timing you quickly pick up on a rivalry between two of the dwarves named Bifit and Bamhul, and a well-placed question over why Bamhul should get first pick for the meal starts a loud verbal argument that quickly leads to a wrestling match among the crazy dwarves. Soon they are all involved and the group easily exits the hollow. You find the trail an hour later and arrive in Anvil the next day."

Example 3: Lost Tower

Our third example is from an unexpected detour the PCs have made into a ruined wizard's tower, when the GM expected the three-player group to head in the opposite direction. These players are experienced and fond of patter, so the GM asks them for a montage. As you'll see, GM embellishment can be a little different when the players have already embellished themselves!

GM set-up: "OK, I admit that I didn't expect you would care about this old tower, and I really have no idea what's in it. But I also want to tackle some bigger things tonight, so I'm suggesting we handle this as a montage, and that way you can have a bit of fun with whatever's here and still have time for the big fight with the . . . whoops, I almost told you! Anyway, like I said, this place is overgrown in strange ivy and it's mostly in ruins. But there's smoke drifting up from somewhere in the ruins."

Problem (player 1): "OK, I can work with that. There doesn't seem to be anyone paying attention to the approaches, because as usual, Krok [the fighter] made a tank-sized noise stumbling up the hill . . . no, be quiet, this is my story, and I'm saying you clanked up the hill. But like I said, it didn't matter. No one reacted to the noise. And then we got to the top of the hill and were about to go into the tower, and all the weird ivy started to glow. Which might not be bad, but there's something really sick and wrong about the color. Over to you, Findel . . ."

GM embellishment: "Yeah. That's right. And when they start to glow, you can see that every seventh leaf on the ivy has sort of rune on it. Later you'll all wonder how you knew it was every seventh leaf, but you just did."

Solution (player 2, Findel's player, not Krok's player!): "Oh, yeah! Wood elf ward ivy! This stuff makes excellent tea when it gets mature. But at the moment all I need to do is quickly touch seven runes in the order of the season, the year, and the official flower of the Court this month. Nailed it."

GM embellishment: "Just out of curiosity, do you explain what you just did?"

Player 2: "No way. My cover story is that I have no idea what's going on at the Court of Stars, so . . . yeah, I just tell them, 'What you have to do is hit the runes that spell *speak friend, and enter*. It's an old elven joke.' And then I snip off a few leaves. They're glowing a great green now. I'll make everybody tea later."

GM: "Right. Wondered if you were going to fess up. What you got next?"

Problem (player 2): "The interior of the tower has been broken up and remodeled by a family or squad of hill giants who tunneled in instead of coming through the ward ivy. They're roasting some people they must have captured somewhere."

Solution (player 3, Krok's player): "It's hammer time! Hill giants make an awful lot of noise as they fall. Turn up the music for a minute, because it's heavy metal Friday and by the time I'm finished with these giants, they'll have knocked down lots of the rest of the tower when they come crashing down. And yeah, you two can fight too, but mostly you were busy pulling the human survivors out of the fire and out of the way of the falling giants."

GM embellishment: "Not all the survivors are human. At least one of them is a drow wearing a cloak that's in style this week at the Court."

Problem (player 3): "Well it seems we've got some pretty badly damaged civilians here. Let's say there are three left alive, counting the drow, but a couple of them are really badly burned. And it's not Krok who's going to be able to keep them alive."

GM embellishment: "The drow woman is only a little hurt, like a broken wrist and bad scrapes. She's trying to keep her companions, a human man and a woman alive, and crying tears of rage and frustration, because she's no magician."

Solution (player 1): This looks bad, because we don't really have enough healing magic to help out like we should, not with Jum [the missing cleric] out. But all the crashing and smashing brought down some storage platforms that the giants had put way up high. I know what healing potions look like and I find three, although one of them looks a bit like an old orc salve. Anyway I get them to the burn victims and I think it's enough to keep them alive."

GM embellishment: "You saved them both. I'll come up with their names in a minute. But I'm just going to cut to the point: Findel, you know how you rolled a 5 with the Elf Queen today? It's now a 6 instead of a 5. You just dealt with the complication, and these people are friends of the Court of Stars, and whatever you might have had coming as a complication later should be something they can help smooth out."

Using Icon Relationship Dice

The icons—and the relationships each character has with them—are a core concept of the *13th Age* RPG. Those relationships work on a story level as players create stories to support the relationships, and on a mechanical level as the players roll icon dice to determine the benefits their PCs get from those relationships. One question that often comes up from both GMs and players is how to use those 5s and 6s during play. Here's some additional advice to consider along with the examples of icon dice use presented in the core rulebook and *13 True Ways*. Some of these thoughts will go into more detail about the icon advantage framework Jonathan and Rob laid out in the core rulebook, while others expand that framework with new approaches or mechanics. Use or ignore these options as you wish.

The following ideas can be used by both GMs and players, whether for long-term campaigns or one-off games. In general, however, icon relationship rolls have the greatest impact in persistent campaigns where story changes can have lasting effects.

When to Roll Icon Dice?

The core rulebook suggests rolling icon dice at the start of every session, or perhaps at the end to set up the story for the next session. But what do you do when every player (or most) rolls one or more advantages? With groups of five or six players, it might mean ten or more advantages to use that session. Some GMs struggle to incorporate every icon result into the session; and if players don't get the benefit they expected, they might feel as if their rolls were wasted. Here are some alternatives.

Lump Multiple Advantages Together

Especially when you have a group of five or six players and are generating double-digit advantages, consider lumping results with the same icon together. This may create story events that affect multiple characters or the whole party.

If a player rolls multiple advantages with the same icon, it's fine to combine them into a greater advantage instead of using each separate roll. Those two 6s with the Dwarf King and his people are one big favor instead of two smaller ones, and three 6s would be a really big favor. As GM, if you see an opportunity where combining a second advantage with the first would be more helpful to the party, ask the player if you could use it that way. They could say no because they have plans for it, but usually they'll go along. Just make sure you follow through and make the advantage better than normal. Creating more powerful advantages than usual is fine so long as any complications are also stronger!

You probably don't want to choose this route every time, because there's a lot to be said for advantages that are tailored to a single character. But if your GMing-brain threw up its metaphorical hands when you saw the number of results that you, or your players, were set to interpret in the next session, this is your escape hatch.

Roll After Full Heal-Up

Another option is to limit the number of results by only rolling icon dice after each full heal-up. For groups that have longer sessions, that might still end up being once per session; but often it will extend to a second (or maybe even a third) session depending on session length. Rolling the dice less can give the GM and players more time to decide how to best use their advantages, especially with time available between sessions to get creative. Of course, if those rolls come up empty, the GM can always ask for more rolls sooner, or rolls for specific icons only again at a relevant story point.

Roll When the Advantages Run Out

Another timing option for icon dice is to let the players roll again only when the group uses the last advantage they gained from the previous icon dice rolls. This guarantees all advantages will be used (and each player with a 5 or 6 gets a chance to shine). The downside is that it might take multiple sessions before the group gets to roll icon dice again, especially if one player hoards their advantages "for when we really need it." Also, GMs who aren't fully comfortable incorporating icon advantages into the game will find that this approach means more story chaos than usual results for groups that renew them often.

No Rolls?

If your table's problem is the opposite of too many icon advantages because players consistently roll too few, don't forget that some icon advantages can be awarded without being rolled by the players. A perfectly good reward to the PCs for completing a quest or doing a service for an iconic servant is to grant them (or those PCs with connections to the icon) a lasting advantage (like rolling a 6) with that icon that the PC holds onto until they use it or some amount of time goes by (usually when they level up). You'll see a lot of that type of reward in the upcoming Battle Scenes books.

WHAT DO THE CONNECTIONS MEAN?

As the core rulebook explains, before you start trying to figure out what advantages and complications to give PCs, make sure you're clear on their iconic relationships and unique stories. After each player has chosen their icon relationships, have them explain the story behind those choices. If a fighter has a negative relationship with the Lich King, learn what is driving that feud. If a cleric has a conflicted relationship with the Diabolist, make sure you know why they sometimes gain her favor, but not always. Those story choices inform the ways in which their 6s and (especially) 5s come into play.

For example, when you learn that the cleric was a former Diabolist cultist who left after being forced to sacrifice her father,

you know that the advantages from that icon probably come from inside knowledge, or from enemies of the icon who are helping the cleric take revenge on the cult. But complicated advantages probably mean she is still in contact with active cultists from her past who have their own agendas, or with former members who are willing to betray the others for a price.

As GM, you should also review the icon relationships with other icons in chapter 1 of the core rulebook if you're playing in the Dragon Empire as written, or think about the connections you've created in a home game with tailored icons. Which icons did the players choose, and who are the enemies and allies of those icons? For example, a ranger with a 2-point positive relationship with the Elf Queen tends to face complications involving the Orc Lord's servants and receives help not only from the Elf Queen, but also from the High Druid's followers and the Emperor's servants. Keeping those allies and enemies in mind helps when you decide to have some faction provide assistance as an advantage or complicated advantage. Even better, have a sheet at hand during the game with a chart listing each icon in the group and their allies and enemies, plus a few possible goals the followers of those icons might have in the game world that relate to the PCs. Then you have some ready-made complication hooks you can flesh out more as needed. (See page 62 for one version of such a sheet.)

Tips on Using Icon Advantages

Since this is a GM's guide, we'll first cover some strategies for using icon advantages in different ways, including how to let the players do half the work. Later, we'll provide some examples of advantages and complications actually used during games that might be enlightening to either GMs or players. But first, a reminder from the core rules.

If you're not sure what enemies and obstacles the PCs will face next, or you want to flavor some generic opposition you've created for the PCs, use their icon rolls to push the story toward an icon (or two). The easy way to do this is to see what advantages the PCs rolled, tally up which icon got the most (5s and 6s both), and flavor the enemies and that session's story toward that icon. In addition, any allies that show up to help thanks to advantages should also be linked to the icon—whether servants of the icon or those of an allied icon—or enemies wishing to do that icon harm and who are willing to help the PCs, depending on the disposition of the PCs toward the icon.

Also remember that if you're not sure what direction to go in a session, you can simply pick the icon that the most PCs have in common and craft the story using the methods we just described. The main difference with this approach is that the PCs won't have any favors to call in this time.

Who's Responsible?

Maybe you take all the responsibility for figuring out what happens with icon advantages. Maybe you share it with the PCs. Here are notes on three possible approaches.

Approach 1: 6s = Players; 5s = GM

As GM, you've got plenty of things to worry about during a game session, and thinking of ways for players to use their icon advantages is something you shouldn't need to do . . . except for complicated advantages. Let the players come up with creative ideas for using their 6s. It's on them, and they'll probably have better ideas than a GM who can only give a sliver of their thought processes to any one player. That doesn't mean you shouldn't remind them that they haven't used an advantage, or make suggestions (or offers) if something seems obvious, or even push for something when the setup is just right (but always with player buy-in). But let them do the creative work most of the time. One caveat to that advice, however, is when you're running a game for players new to *13th Age*. In such cases, helping the players understand what advantages actually mean by offering more suggestions makes sense.

Complicated advantages (5s), on the other hand, are a GM's bread and butter. If a player suggests a use for one of these advantages, that's fine, but you should be immediately thinking of ways to twist it or turn it into an offer of help for something else, either immediately, or down the road, or the attention using that advantage will bring. Even better is when the player suggests a complication, since most of the time it will be worse that whatever you were planning. Just remember, it's fine if you adjust it to fit knowledge about the campaign only you have, or even reject it outright if it's too much (but try to find ways to say yes to player ideas if you can so the player doesn't clam up).

As GM, when you see a good opportunity to use a player's 5, most likely you've also thought of the twist you can add thanks to the complication at the same time. But remember, 5s aren't about screwing a player over, they're about complicating the story for that PC and the group in an interesting way. Instead of the PCs getting to their goal or directing the narrative in the way they would prefer, they now have to take a detour to get there, and that detour should be full of fun as well. Some detours from complications might even make the PCs choose to let go of their original goal to follow the new path.

For example, the PCs are trying to track down a rogue who stole something from an icon that one or more of the group has a positive relationship with, in this case the Emperor, and aren't having much luck. One PC with a 5 with the Orc Lord decides to use it to find the thief (suggested by the player). The GM smiles: they would eventually need to find the thief, and now they're getting his location from an Orc Lord contact, a half-orc witch doctor in the wilds who lives next to the Valley of Bones. To get the information they want, of course the witch doctor will require them to retrieve a relic—an orc general's skull—from the valley, which has various dangers and spirit guardians they must face. That complication just generated one or two battles' worth of adventure. And maybe the witch doctor uses the skull to bring back that orc general, who, of course, the PCs will have to face at some point.

Making the PCs go retrieve an item or ask for knowledge from an NPC as the complication from a 5 is always a good way to generate new adventure leads, especially for GMs who like to be surprised each session and don't plan out storylines.

Approach 2: All Results = GM

With this approach, all icon roll results are yours, for world building and getting players unstuck when the game stalls. The GM uses the results—whether they were rolled at the beginning of the session or beforehand—as inspiration for how the night's adventure will go, introducing new campaign arcs, or adding twists to existing arcs. The GM then either uses the remaining icon results as a sort of "divine intervention" pool to help the players when their PCs are well and truly hosed, or allows them to expire unused. If you go this route, however, know that you'll have to do more record-keeping in tracking the rolls. You'll also be taking some power away from the players for creating surprising storylines.

Approach 3: All Results = Players

We've seen a player-driven approach to icon results described in several places, and Wade uses it in his own campaign. Give players who roll 5s or 6s physical tokens to represent those results—ideally something eye-catching such as shiny coins, cards, or the official icon tokens coming soon from Campaign Coins—to remind them that they have an unused resource available. The players can then "spend" those benefits to overcome extraordinary challenges, telling the GM how their relationship with the icon gives them the necessary edge in that situation.

The GM can also set up challenges that take this resource into account, asking the players if they want to spend an appropriate icon advantage now to get information or overcome an obstacle, or hold on to it until later—with the knowledge that if they don't use the result by the end of the game, it expires. This approach is similar to point spends in games based on the GUMSHOE investigative system. When a player spends a 5, the GM will either introduce a complication on the spot or let the player know that they will have to pay the price for this advantage at some point.

GMs using this method should be prepared to be continually surprised, and maybe have to stretch at times to link narratives together when a player takes the story in a wild direction.

More on Complications

Another great option with complicated advantages (5s) is to offer the PC with it help when the group is stuck, but at a cost. Tell them the cost up front if you have something in mind, or call it a "favor to be called-in later" if you need to. At that point, it's all about tough choices for the player: something good now for something bad or difficult later.

For example, the PCs find a portal they think leads to a location they need to go to, but it's not active. After a few failed tries to activate it, the wizard with a conflicted Diabolist relationship sees an imp servitor pop into existence nearby. The imp sometimes provides assistance, but always at a cost. The imp offers to provide the activation words, but requires the wizard to retrieve an object from the place beyond the portal and deliver it to the imp. The item probably increases the Diabolist's power in some way, so now the wizard's player must choose to use that 5 or find a different solution.

When you come up with a plan on how to use a complicated advantage, either tell the player up front what the cost will be to gain the advantage, or if you're not sure or you want to keep the information secret, record it for later. But when you do finally spring the complication on the players, remember to inform them that the event or situation causing trouble was due to their use of the complicated advantage. It reinforces the consequences of using 5s and lets the players know you're not forgetting about them. If at all possible, try to use that complication within a few full heal-ups, or by the end of the level, or there's a chance everyone will forget about it.

Taking Advantage of Advantages

Iconic advantages are usually story related. The PCs are searching for something or someone, need information, are facing an obstacle of some sort, need help defeating a powerful enemy, or require similar assistance. It's usually not hard to come up with NPCs, functionaries, helpers, or other followers of the icons to provide that assistance when the group is in a city or other location inhabited by people. But when they're deep in the underworld, inside a dormant volcano, or out in the wilds, justifying some NPC showing up can be more difficult within the framework of the story.

The core book gives a few options, such as flashbacks or magical aid already given. Another option it lists that can be a real boon for the GM is magical spirits. Sprites, souls of those who have passed, overworld spirits, imps and demons, messenger spells in humanoid form, elemental creatures, talking beasts, and similar entities are a great way to gift magic items, provide help, or pass on information to the PCs to fulfill an advantage, and are usually easily explained in the game world. Even if the campaign is low magic, some types of supernatural entities probably have a place in the campaign. And if the icons are able to use those creatures to help the PCs, problem solved.

If none of those options fit the story, and sentient or semi-sentient magic items are a part of the campaign, they are another option for a GM when information or some type of general assistance is required. Perhaps those items have been around for a while and experienced some things or have some latent power that's been waiting for the proper trigger. Maybe an icon can use them to pass on information, or maybe they just provide it on their own, with the GM flavoring it to the icon in play. Sentient, talking items work best for this, but an item's wielder could receive an image or feeling from it that yields valuable information. Or maybe that dragon shield that has never said anything before suddenly starts spilling its guts. It might not do it again, but the advantage allowed it to help this one time, or maybe there's now a link to the Great Gold Wyrm there. Creative options for fulfilling advantages are there for those willing to look.

Another option that works in a more magical game is iconic tattoos. Perhaps the PC with the advantage has had the symbol of the icon tattooed or inscribed on their flesh at some point in the past. When they need special help, the magic of the tattoo/inscription flares, creating a link with the icon's people. If you go this route, treat the tattoos or markings as a generalized form of magic that don't take up chakras. Or at least, the ones that do have other powers associated with them (we'd love to see what type of magic tattoos people come up with).

Finally, keep in mind that all advantages don't need to hold equal weight. Perhaps an initial session's rolls dictate the main iconic antagonist in the narrative. Future icon rolls don't have to steal the thunder from the icon once you've settled on a primary storyline. They just induce bouts of flavor from the other icons that help the PCs overcome the challenges set by the main narrative. For example, icons rolls for the start of a new adventure set up the Orc Lord as the main antagonist for the narrative. During the next session, the necromancer rolls three 5s or 6s with the Lich King. Those should have an impact on the Orc Lord story, but shouldn't necessarily change it to a Lich King story mid-stream. Maybe the necromancer calls up a dead host to help fight an orc horde between the PCs and their goal, meaning they just sneak around, no fighting involved. Of course, if there's a perfect story fit, maybe what seemed to be an Orc Lord story was just the Lich King pulling certain strings all along, and both icons have a place in that narrative. But that's the GM's call.

Mechanical Benefits for Advantages

The core rulebook generally discusses iconic advantages as things that help PCs overcome story obstacles, provide information, or perhaps avoid fights before they start. They weren't necessarily designed to provide mechanical benefits to a PC. But sometimes a player wants to use an advantage during battle to help overcome an enemy, to survive the battle, or to help an ally in some way. Unless both the players and GM agree to this type of usage as standard, it's probably best to limit it to special story circumstances. But doing so isn't wrong. There's no reason an advantage couldn't turn a hard DC into a normal one, or make the rest of a mob of mooks flee the battle, or provide a PC with a +5 damage bonus on ranged attacks against a special foe, as long as the GM is okay with it.

Having advantages provide mechanical benefits can also solve another issue: losing unused advantages. Some groups might allow advantages to carry over, but the standard method is to have them simply reset when new rolls occur. Players always

want to be efficient in their use of advantages, but sometimes the opportunity or creativity isn't there, and they get wasted. One way to solve this issue, if everyone is on board, is to house rule that an advantage can always be converted into a mechanical benefit. If you go this route, make sure the benefit is small, since too many advantages can turn a hard battle into a cakewalk. If you go this route, make sure you continue to introduce complications for 5s used this way, probably some event during that battle that makes things dicey for the group, like an enemy reroll or damage on a miss.

Here are a few examples of advantages converted to mechanical benefits that might work: reroll a d20, reroll all damage dice, gain a +2 attack bonus before a roll, temporary hit points fitting the tier and level, a small extra effect or condition applied to a spell or power that hits, and so on. If you like, feel free to tell your group that you're going to use mechanical advantages this way on a trial basis, and see how it affects the game balance. You can always revert if it's too much. Of course, the best way to ensure advantages get used normally instead of as mechanical boons is to make sure that the advantages have cool, helpful, story-changing effects when the players use them.

Examples of Using Advantages and Complications

The *13 True Ways* rulebook has good examples in the city section of how to apply icon advantages for each icon in that city, but here are some examples showing various methods of fulfilling random advantages that we've used in our games. Perhaps they'll give you, or your players, some ideas on the possibilities for icon advantages.

- ***Complicated advantage using a flashback and gift (5):*** The PCs are sneaking up a ridge to flank a war party of orcs and ogres camped on high ground, when an ogre walks to the edge in sight of them. Everyone makes their skill check to hide except the barbarian, who fumbles it, which means alerting the ogre and the camp. Instead, the sorcerer uses a 5 with the Elf Queen, describing a one-use magic gem he was given recently that creates a limited illusion. And so, the ogre sees only ferns and rocks below. As a simple complication, the ogre proceeds to relieve himself on the "rocks" below, spraying the PCs with ogre scent, which comes into play later when the camp wolves smell the PCs. It wasn't a big story event, but it created a group joke for a few levels.
- ***Complicated advantage (5):*** A rogue with an assassin background takes jobs from his guild (run by the Merchant King icon, a mob-like offshoot of the Dwarf King). One of the jobs went south and the mark takes a hit out on him. During the next battle, an assassin tries to kill the rogue, resorting to burning a building down with him inside, but he and the PCs escape. Later, the rogue confronts his assassin, but instead of fighting, the player uses two 5s with the Merchant King to convince the assassin to join forces, so the PC can start his own network of killers. It's all good, except the GM-provided complication is that the assassin needs to fulfill her contract first, so she tells the rogue it's a deal if he leaves town for a month to make it look good and provides proof of the kill, a valuable ring the rogue recently acquired. Now the rogue has a new contact, and possibly an NPC to help him on "missions."
- ***Mechanical Advantage (6):*** A necromancer with a conflicted relationship with the Gatekeeper, a variant Lich King icon, is facing a rival and needs information from the man. The battle is difficult, and party survival is touch and go. The rival necromancer is near death, but the PCs can't afford to risk keeping him alive to get the information. So the necromancer uses a 6 with the Gatekeeper to empower his scythe attack; when he kills his rival, the player suggests the man's soul is trapped and at the whim of the necromancer PC. The rival can gain his release to the next world by revealing one secret. The necromancer uses this leverage to learn the secret, which helps the group avoid a later ambush as well.
- ***Complicated advantage, long-term complication chosen after the session (5):*** The party discovers a woman held in stasis at the bottom of an old elven ziggurat that also holds trapped demons the group has been fighting. A powerful ritual kept her trapped and unaffected by time, and removing it safely without causing her harm is a ridiculously hard DC. A cleric of the dark gods (Crusader relationship) uses two 5s with the Crusader to bring down the ritual without rolling. The woman is freed, and lies, saying that she is a dark cleric of a previous servant of the dark gods (she's been in stasis for an age). She thanks them for their help and travels with them out of the place. Later, since two 5s were used to free her, the GM determines the complication to be that she is a shapechanged demon, trapped within the ziggurat by the dark elves who couldn't kill her. Now freed, she learns about the party, helps them in one battle (in human form), then flees during the next battle. Later in the campaign she shows up, transforms into a marilith, and is on the arms of her master, a demon who is the hated enemy of the PC cleric. This one was a longer-term complication that took a few levels to come to completion.
- ***Complicated advantage, complication arising from a previous session (5):*** In the process of repelling a kobold attack on a mining village, the party wounded a young dragon, causing it to flee. At the beginning of a later session, a PC rolls a 5 with the Three. The icon reveals that the dragon is hiding in the forest of a previous High Druid, and the Orc Lord's forces are seeking to capture and enslave it as a weapon of war. If the party wishes the help of the Three, they must pledge to enter the awakened and angry forest, save the wounded dragon from the Orc Lord's minions, and deliver it safely to the Three's followers. Depending on the outcome of this quest, the PCs might gain a new ally and an opportunity to use the *13th Age* dragon riding rules!

ALTERNATIVE ICON SYSTEMS

The systems that follow aren't how we do things. But we know GMs who roll this way, so maybe you'll want to experiment with one of these optional systems.

Every Roll Counts

Using this optional rule, every result on an icon die produces an in-game effect. When a player rolls icon dice, they take the single highest result for each icon.

6: The PC gains an advantage.

5: The PC gains an advantage with a complication.

4: The icon doesn't intervene, but gives the PC information relevant to the adventure. This information is accurate, though it might be incomplete.

3: The icon subjects the PC to a normal skill check in exchange for a broad hint related to the adventure. Failure results in misinformation that delays the group, or makes the next battle slightly more difficult (one extra creature of the PCs' level).

2: The icon subjects the PC to a hard skill check in exchange for information related to the adventure. This information is mostly wrong or misleading, but it contains an element of truth. Failure is the same as option 3 above.

1: The PC messed up badly and must now do a job for the icon with no reward. If the PC refuses to do the job, the party suffers a campaign loss as described in the rules for fleeing a battle.

Icon Disadvantages

GMs running a grittier campaign than the default "high adventure" tone of *13th Age* might want to add an element of danger to icon relationships by introducing the concept of icon disadvantages. This works especially well in dark fantasy settings where the icons are indifferent at best to the fate of adventurers.

On an icon die result of 1, the PC's relationship with the icon works against them somehow, whether mechanically or in terms of the story. Often that's because the icon's enemies draw a bead on the player character, but sometimes the icon or other followers of the icon are the problematic element of the equation.

On a result of 2, the PC suffers some misfortune related to the icon, but gets an advantage that almost makes up for it.

If you use only these two adjustments, icon relationships look pretty close to a zero-sum game. You could forgive your players for saying "No, no, I don't need to roll any icon relationship dice today. That's OK." And that's bad.

So if you use the idea that 1s and 2s can create icon disadvantages, it's better to make 5s almost entirely good for the PC. The complicated problem now lives in the 2. And it's a bit worse than the 5 used to be. But both the 5 and 6 are purely positive, or as positive as anything gets in these dark fantasy streets.

BUILDING BETTER BATTLES

The *13th Age* core rulebook gives GMs the basics for building battles, including the Monster Equivalents chart for handling the math side of things, and some advice on building "unfair" battles. In this section, we'll expand on those ideas and provide a deeper look into how to craft fun, memorable battles.

Battles are only a part of the *13th Age* roleplaying experience, but it is an F20 game, and fights are part of its DNA. Sometimes the players' actions or the direction of the story (too many 5s on icon rolls!) will lead to an unexpected battle that can't be avoided through stealth, negotiation, or other means. Because the GM has to construct them on the fly, and simpler is usually easier, these battles are often not especially memorable, and end up as filler in between more important scenes. But when a GM has time to plan, knowing where the heroes' path will most likely lead, and who's going to be in their way looking for fight—that's when they can give their players a battle to truly remember, perhaps even one that will define a PC or take the campaign in a new direction.

So what makes a *13th Age* battle memorable? The obvious answer is how the fight applies to the characters' stories. Some battles will just involve the PCs doing normal hero stuff: Exploring, finding trouble, and trying to stay alive when they encounter enemies that want to eat them or kill them. However, when you personalize a battle for one or more of the PCs by challenging them with enemies linked to them through their iconic connections, backgrounds, or *uniques*, you immediately gain the players' attention.

A battle against a group of generic gnolls, for example, is a lot less interesting to the players than a fight against the Demonfiends, the Diabolist-worshiping gnoll pack who are sworn enemies of the wood elf ranger PC with a negative relationship with that icon, and who has a background called "Demonfiend hunter" but left it up to the GM to figure out what that means. That battle has personal impact for the ranger's player. It probably also opens up new adventure options, either from the ranger wanting to know where the gnoll pack came from and how it found the party, or for you to expand upon if you see that the battle caught the ranger player's interest.

So what goes into building those memorable battles? Outlined below are key ideas to keep in mind while creating fights for the PCs, including choice of theme, battle difficulty, monster type, level, and strength, and what tactics they might employ. While a lot of this advice is directed at the battles you can plan ahead of time, you can still draw upon these strategies when you're slapping together a battle-on-the-fly or running a one-shot adventure.

CHOOSE A THEME

For a home campaign, you know the players and their PCs best, so you should understand what types of enemies the players like to face, how tactical they are in combat, and—most importantly—what icon relationships and *uniques* the PCs have that will best link to the battles and enemies they'll face. Of course, that doesn't mean you can't occasionally throw curveballs at them to take them out of their comfort zones, but you need to gain their trust before hitting them with a battle they think they won't enjoy. So it helps to decide what a battle's theme will be, which helps you then choose enemies, terrain, and how tough the battle should be.

The *13th Age* icon relationships and rolls are great for setting a theme, since player icon choices should help you generate ideas about what types of monsters to use. If the battle is the result of icon interactions (including direct representatives or enemies who fall under an icon's sphere of influence) and/or complications from icon dice, the theme is probably obvious. For example, the PCs have a necromancer who's out to stop the Lich King, and they defeat a lesser vampire who bargains for its (un) life by telling the party about a hidden vault of death priests. You now have your theme: the PCs will be involved in one or more battles with Lich King death priests and their undead minions. Once you have a direction to go, you can find existing resources that fit that theme, or create the battles yourself.

But maybe the PCs' current course doesn't have any icon involvement. What then? Well, most likely the group is pursuing a storyline that involves one of their *uniques*. You know the stories they want to tell based on those *uniques*, and you should have some idea about the elements you want to weave into the campaign, which should inform your choice of theme and what sort of battle the PCs will face to achieve what they want. If one of the PCs has a *unique* story involving retrieving a family heirloom from the drow raiders who killed his family, and the PCs are following a sub-group of those raiders, your theme for the next battle might be any of the following: the PCs encounter a drow raiding party that has broken off from the main group to attack a small settlement; the PCs must face a group of underworld monsters that pick up their scent and attack as the heroes descend into the depths; or perhaps the PCs encounter a band of deep forest denizens who won't let them pass through their lands to pursue the drow that recently passed through. At that point, you know the story and the enemies, and you'll just need to do some stat work for the enemies you choose and pick the terrain.

In a similar vein, your theme choice might revolve around a background of one or more of the PCs. While backgrounds aren't as strong as *uniques* thematically, they still tell stories about the PCs and can be mined for drama the same way. For example, a PC rogue who's a "disgraced former monk of the Golden Temple" has provided theme gold for you, since current members of that temple might be hunting the character. Look for opportunities to take advantage of backgrounds involving groups, organizations, or entities that a player has created and set into a conflicting relationship.

Finally, the story might come to a point where icon connections, unique storylines, or backgrounds are not currently driving the action. Perhaps the PCs are lingering in a town, waiting for the next adventure to slap them in the face, or their current location or the geography dictates what types of dangers are present. Your theme might be "battle to kick off the next storyline I want to introduce with a bandit king of the Prince of Shadows" or "traveling the Midland Sea is now dangerous." For the former, you decide to have street thugs try to rob the PCs in a small town. The thug attack will lead to deeper connections with the bandit king and more iconic storylines. For the latter, you've decided that the Emperor (or Archmage?) is having trouble keeping the sea calm, and attacks on ship travelers by sahuagin will set up a new storyline where the heroes help that icon regain control over the sea . . . probably in opposition to the Diabolist.

No matter which option is driving the story, knowing the theme of your battle will help you make the other choices for the battle like what enemies to use, how difficult the battle will be, and what outcomes might result from it.

Choose the Difficulty

You have a theme, so you know the feel you want for your battle. Based on that, it's time to figure out how tough to make the battle. Most of the time, you'll want to build a standard battle, one that presents an equal fight for the PCs as explained in the core rules. What a "standard battle" is will vary from group to group, however. If you've got players who know the system, and know how to get the most out of their powers and group synergies, a normal battle will barely challenge them unless they have terrible dice luck. You probably want to design standard battles at 25% to 50% tougher than normal, as if there were one to three more PCs present depending on the party size. On the flip side, if your group is more interested in roleplaying and wants quick fights, doesn't include PCs who are built for combat effectiveness, doesn't know the system well yet, or isn't interested in challenging fights for whatever reason, keep the battles at the standard baseline described in the core rules, or even tone them back, assuming one less PC.

Once you have your baseline standard battle, continue to use that until circumstances change. That doesn't mean you always throw a standard battle at your group, however. It's important to mix things up. Some battles might be much easier because of smart choices by the players, use of icon advantages, and other factors. Other times, especially for key story points, it might be a fight for survival or the PCs are trying to defeat special enemies. Feel free to throw a double-strength battle at them (double whatever "standard" is), or even a triple-strength battle for truly special scenes. If you do build a triple-strength battle, it should probably be for a fight right before leveling up, or a battle against a long-time villain, or for a similarly dramatic scene, since there's a good chance of one or more of the PCs going down. Such battles should always have a dramatic outcome for the PCs and the story to make them feel special and to provide a reward for a life-or-death encounter.

Of course, you can always make a battle tougher if things are going too easy for the PCs, or tone a fight back if you realize it's too much for them, or bad rolls have swayed things. Adding or subtracting an extra normal monster or two usually won't sway the battle too strongly in one direction, especially if that enemy is a troop or a group of mooks. Perhaps some enemies flee, or go for reinforcements. Also, the flee rules are a good way to let PCs in over their heads get out of trouble, with story changing consequences (and perhaps a few GM taunts).

One other useful trick if you want to challenge your group with a stronger battle but aren't sure if it might be too much for them is to hold back a few of the enemies. Introduce the foes in waves, with half or two-thirds of the enemies immediately starting the fight, then the remainder joining in after a round or two if the PCs are doing well (and when the escalation die will help more). You can either bring the extras in when it feels right, or choose before the battle that the extras will come at a specific time, such as at the start of the third round, or when the escalation die reaches 2. This timing method is also a good way to reward or penalize PCs who succeed or fail on skill checks leading up to the battle.

One other thing to keep in mind with battle difficulty. If time is limited for your sessions, there's nothing wrong with pitting the PCs against back-to-back double-strength battles. Those fights tend to take a little longer, but you still save time by cutting out two full battles if you follow the normal "four battles per full heal-up" rule from the core book. There's nothing wrong with that, but remember to change things up sometimes as noted previously.

Adjust for Terrain

When you use terrain in your battles (see Incorporating Terrain into Battles on page 36), make sure to adjust the difficulty of the battle as well if the terrain will affect combat. Usually, it's best to make it harder or easier as if there were one more or one less PC in the battle, depending on the terrain and types of effects. Of course, as a nasty GM you could just add it and not change the battle difficulty, telling the players that it's up to them to negate or take advantage of the terrain. Your call.

Choose the Enemies

The types of enemies and monsters you choose for a battle based on theme and difficulty will go a long ways toward making dynamic, interesting battles that players will remember. You know roughly how many points worth of monsters you'll use based on the difficulty you chose, and you know what type of enemies you want to have in the battle based on theme and iconic storylines, so now you need to pick enemies that will fit. The following choices all go hand-in-hand when choosing enemies at this point. These suggestions are focused on groups of four to six PCs; adjust suggested numbers up or down based on your group's size.

Monster Roles & Ability Combinations

You've got your theme, so now you need to pick enemies that fit that story. Certain types of creatures will make more sense for the situation than others, you just have to decide how you want it to play out. Is it an ambush by the enemies? A random meeting? Are the enemies intelligent, or dumb, hungry beasts? The location of the battle should be a consideration to the types of enemies too; monstrous beasts don't make sense in an urban setting (usually), and halfling bandits probably don't work in orc-infested lands (usually). Once you have an idea of what types of enemies you'll use, you're ready to pick roles (though don't be afraid to mix roles; different stories can support odd groupings after all).

In general, it's best to use enemies with different roles, to vary the types of attacks they have and to force the PCs to use different strategies against the enemies. Unless the story dictates it, try to avoid throwing a group of enemies that all have the same role at the PCs. A room full of troops makes sense once in a while, but gives little variety. All leaders and they probably have too few allies to use their abilities on. All wreckers and you might thrash the PCs too hard, or all they do is deal damage, which the PCs might have ways to mitigate easily (or plenty of healing). All blockers and the battle will drag out. All archers, and they'll be easy targets for the PCs to engage and lock down. All spoilers can work sometimes, but you might go crazy trying to track all of the effects they put on the PCs.

Mixed-role groups also tend to have synergies with each other. Look over your options and see what goes best together. A caster role might have an attack that makes enemies vulnerable, while the troops with it deal extra damage against vulnerable foes. A group of spoilers might have fire resistance, and a leader has a hellfire attack that targets all creatures, but will only do half damage to its allies most of the time due to the resistance. Mixing creature types is also useful here, because you get more roles to select from to find combinations. Sure the hobgoblin captain should have some goblin troops to command, but maybe she has a pet hellbeast spoiler that has some nifty power to give the PCs trouble.

If the enemies include a leader or caster, you should also add in blockers, troops, or mooks that can intercept the PCs. If you use archers, they'll either need terrain advantages to avoid the PCs, or you should include troops and mooks as interceptors (but not for troops with ranged attacks, for example, who are fine with getting off one ranged attack and then entering melee). If you use spoilers, what are their tricks? Most spoilers benefit from having allies that seem more dangerous, such as a band of troops or a nasty wrecker, giving them time to make attacks that deal ongoing damage or put conditions on enemies, which can add up as the battle rages. For example, if you want to have a cunning imp in the battle who can deliver verbal barbs to go along with his physical ones, adding a frenzy demon wrecker that can tear the PCs up will probably grab their attention first.

Example build: Let's use the Lich King death priest example from the theme section and decide to make the first battle tougher than standard, but not fully double-strength, since the PCs are entering a location the priests have had time to make defensible and they're intelligent. You have five 4th level PCs, so you set the difficulty at the equivalent of seven 4th level PCs (two above a standard battle). The death priests are the focus of the battle, so you'll include a few of them, and they're casters (and the "bosses" too). Casters are better with support, so you decide that they should have undead troops who protect them as guards. Finally, the death priests have animated some undead flying skulls, mooks that will pester the PCs freely and can get past interceptors to reach non-melee characters.

Now that you know what monster roles the PCs will face, decide how strong you want to make the enemies, choosing their level and strength. If you're only using pre-created creatures from the books, those options will be set and your choices more limited. Experiment with creating your own stat blocks to craft monsters that fit the needs of each battle and story.

Monster Level

The core rules talk about monster levels and how you should vary them instead of always throwing equivalent levels at the PCs. That's solid advice, but there's more to consider. In general, you should avoid using enemies that are less than two levels below the PCs' level. First, the Monster Equivalents chart doesn't support it (for a reason), and second, those enemies will have a tough time hitting the PCs without great rolls, so they'll be mostly useless. You could build an occasional battle with enemies of three or more levels below the PCs if you want to use them as chattel, or if you want to show the PCs how far they've come ("remember how tough fighting kobolds was at 2nd level; we just mowed those creeps down like grass"). If they aren't mixed with tougher foes, you might not want to even call it a battle, since the heroes probably won't be spending any real resources to overcome their enemies.

On the other side, be careful about throwing enemies at the PCs that are too many levels above them. The core book chart doesn't go past four levels at adventurer tier, five levels at champion tier, and six levels at epic tier for a reason. Higher-level enemies hit more often and are harder to hit and kill, obviously, but the biggest issue is their damage output. One hit will often nearly drop a PC so many levels lower, and a critical hit against a PC at less than full strength has a good chance of taking them straight to death at negative half their maximum hit points. We won't say you should never present such a powerful enemy, but if you do, let the players know how deadly those blows are before the battle starts.

For example, if you are throwing a hill giant at a group of 1st level PCs, you could foreshadow the battle by having them hear tales of a vicious giant in the area and have people say that if you see it, just run. Or immediately before the battle starts, you could describe the giant's approach, as the PCs see it chop a wide log in half with one swipe of its axe as it walks toward them. Or if your group doesn't mind metagaming, simply tell them how much damage the giant's attack does. Establish the threat early so they know what they're facing, and then let them choose their fate, though it never hurts to build in some outs with such high-level enemies, like having the giant ask for a toll instead of attacking, or giving the PCs allies or some other help that evens the odds.

When sending too-tough enemies at the PCs, you can also use other tricks to give the PCs a chance. Reduce the enemy's "book stats" by a level or two and call it a runt for its type, or give the standard monster some weaknesses. For example, this hill giant is actually old and half blind: it has the same hit points, but it takes a –4 penalty to attacks and all defenses. It's now dangerous, but not quite as deadly, making it a great final boss fight for a group of 1st level PCs who are about to level up.

In general, sticking with the suggested level ranges in relation to the PCs will mean everyone at the table has more fun. Higher-level enemies are stronger, and will stick around longer, and lower-level ones will die quicker. It's also not hard to adjust a monster's stats up or down a level or two if you want to use an existing creature but it needs a slight adjustment to fit the situation. *13 True Ways* explains how to do that, or you could keep it really simple, using the base stats in the core book for the level you want and keeping the abilities the same.

One last point about picking monster levels. Every rule can be broken, and throwing the PCs against a much stronger enemy who threatens to kill them unless they serve it (and who can carry through with the threat) is an old GM trick and a good way to introduce an iconic enemy boss that the players will all quickly begin to hate. Don't do it too often, make sure the enemy gives the PCs plenty of opportunities to stand down since it wants them to serve it, and when the PCs are higher level, let them pit themselves against their hated master for a little payback.

We'll discuss how strong to make enemies in the next section, which goes hand-in-hand with monster level.

Monster Strength

Choosing whether the enemies will be normal, double-strength, triple-strength, or mooks also depends on the theme, difficulty, and what levels you chose for the monster (and truly, level, strength, and role all go hand-in-hand to determine the points you use to build the battle). First, look at which creatures are leading the enemies, if any. Sometimes it'll just be a group of equal foes with no leader, but most of the time you'll have one creature who leads the others (or speaks for them at least). This leader (we'll call them a boss) is often a servant of one of the icons the PCs are pitted against. It's not always a creature with the leader role, either, and you could have multiple bosses in a battle (though we'd suggest no more than two). It could be the biggest lizardman warrior (a wrecker), a half-elf sorcerer (a caster) leading a group of bandits, or a dragonic assassin (a spoiler) overseeing a troop of kobolds—basically someone who speaks for the enemy, directs them, and will probably be the focus of the PCs' attacks. More than likely, this creature has a name that you've given it. Decide if you want your boss to have some staying power in the battle or not.

If you want the boss to last longer, make it higher level than the PCs and/or double-strength, or even triple-strength, representing the fact that this one has risen above its fellows and managed to stay alive so far. It's likely that the PCs will try to take out the strongest opponents first during a battle, especially ones that assist or heal their allies, since it will hasten the battle in the PCs' favor to remove such enemies. Making the boss stronger will mitigate player focus somewhat as the team tries to gang up on that foe. It also keeps your mouthpiece as GM around longer.

You also might want a boss who doesn't last as long. For example, the boss has a powerful ability that could hurt the PCs badly, so you're okay with that creature lasting only a few rounds. And if the PCs don't get to that boss, it's going to be a tough fight. Or maybe you want to build the battle so that the boss isn't really the enemy that's going to bring the hurt to the PCs, but rather is a target to distract them. For example, the goblin shaman is annoying and talks tough, but her attack really isn't that damaging. But while the PCs are trying to eradicate her, the shaman's two double-strength bugbear bodyguards will rip them to shreds. It all ties in to the theme and feel you want to present the players with the battle, and it's important to vary the threats from battle to battle so the PCs can't always use the same strategy to tear down your nice opponents before they even get a chance to have some fun.

Once you know how tough your boss is, if you have one, you can move on to the other enemies in the battle. Here are some additional suggestions for enemies with different roles, though you should always design battles to fit the feel you want for that fight.

Usually, make non-boss casters and archers about the PCs' level (or a level above at champion-tier, and perhaps two levels above at epic-tier, adjustments you can assume through the rest of this section). They'll have minions to intercept PCs coming for them, or take advantage of terrain or movement abilities to avoid damage and stick around. And if they let themselves get engaged, well, they should go down quick like the squishies they are. If you choose to make them much stronger or higher level, there's a good chance that the PCs will take a lot more damage during the battle or suffer a lot of conditional effects. Sometimes that's okay based on the theme, but in general it can make a battle too swingy.

Keep blockers and troops around the same level as the PCs, plus or minus a level or two. Since troops tend to be the most-common enemies, making them much weaker or stronger will make the battle go quicker or last longer. Having a single high-level blocker as a bodyguard to an enemy that's easier to kill works fine, but don't make a group of blockers too strong or it will extend the duration of the battle significantly since blockers tend to have higher defenses or be able to reduce damage, and before you know it everyone is reduced to using basic attacks and bored.

Wreckers dish out punishment but aren't usually tricky and often have lower defenses. A lot of battles will have a single higher-level or extra-strength wrecker who gives the party trouble, but a group of same-level ones can be just as devastating if there are a lot of them and they gang up on one PC. Generally, we suggest not using more than one or two in any battle unless you have a specific situation in mind that makes sense for the story. If you want to use multiple wreckers at high levels or extra strength, be very careful, because they can quickly drop a PC, and it only takes a couple of characters failing death saves to take the battle into TPK land. In that case, don't give them too many supporting allies that can diffuse the PCs' attacks against them, keeping those high-damage dealers around.

How strong you make spoilers totally depends on their abilities. Some spoilers are much deadlier than others, especially if they have abilities that weaken or stun, or last-gasp or death effects that can potentially take PCs out of the action for rounds (or the entire battle). If you use a single spoiler that is a key piece

of the battle's theme, feel free to make it much stronger or higher level (or both). But rein in using a lot of spoilers that are stronger than the PCs. Besides making fights deadly, they can also slow things down as you're trying to track various conditions on PCs and other effects. For that reason alone, limiting yourself to three spoilers or fewer per battle is generally a good idea, or even a single one if you've got a complex creature like a couatl. Of course, if you're the type of GM who loves complex battles and tracking all the various elements, go for it!

Usually, you don't need to worry too much about mooks; they're designed to be cannon fodder. They're also best if they are no more than two levels higher than the PCs, and even better if the same level or lower. You want the PCs to mow them down, wasting time on them while the tougher enemies keep making nasty attacks (unless, of course, you design a battle where the mooks are the real threat, but another enemy, perhaps a blocker with high defenses, seems like the real foe). Mooks are designed to be simple, often having only a single attack, and maybe one special ability, if any. That makes them easy to run during a battle. Keep in mind, however, that since you'll often have large mobs (since five mooks of equal level are the equivalent of one standard monster), that means a lot of attack rolls in the early rounds before they start to go down. Those rolls take time and slow things down a bit. Usually it's not a problem, but a couple of options to speed things up if you do have more than ten mooks is to make one roll for each mob (all members hit or miss based on that roll), or even better, break the mob into smaller groups of around three, multiplying any damage by the amount in that group. It skews their effectiveness based on how you roll, but it's quicker.

While we suggest keeping mooks near the PCs' level, there is one GM trick to be aware of with higher-level mooks. Use them as the "elite guards" for a boss. They'll be hard to hit and will hit the PCs often, but their damage is lower and they'll go down easy. Tough, but not too tough. The key is to make sure most of the other enemies besides the boss are around the same level as the PCs or lower to keep the battle reasonable.

Tactics and Events that Affect Monster Choices

How the players approach the battle and what actions they take during it should dictate the enemy's tactics, based on how intelligent those enemies are. But it may be that you see the fight as a hit-and-run affair by the enemies, or decide the leader will flee once staggered, or decide to bring only half the enemies in the first wave, and the other half once the escalation die is 2+, or even that an earthquake will suddenly send everyone in the battle running for cover in the fourth round. Take into account any choice that will limit the enemies in a battle, whether they flee early, arrive late, or are made weaker (or stronger) in some other way. If the tactic or event has a direct outcome on the battle, adjust monster strength up or down accordingly to account for it.

For example, you decide that the bandit leader Blackjack will flee the fight once he's staggered, to go warn his crime boss leader. Since the battle's boss will only fight for half a battle, you can choose between counting Blackjack as half-a-monster in the battle building math, or increasing Blackjack's level or strength so that he gets to have an impact before he runs off.

Adjustments During Battle

An important part of keeping battles fun and engaging for the players is to constantly make adjustments as situations change. Of course, it's fine to let the dice roll as they may and see what happens. But sometimes neither you nor the players are rolling very well, or one side or the other is rolling too well. Or you designed what you thought was a tough battle, but the monsters are more vicious than you realized and are tearing the PCs apart, or they're less effective than you thought and hardly having any effect. Luckily, the fleeing rule lets the players get out of most jams caused by bad luck, but forcing the PCs to flee isn't always the most fun option, especially when you know it was bad design on your part. A different option is to change monsters, stats, or rolls on the fly.

Bad Dice/Good Dice

When you're rolling well, haven't missed with any attack in two rounds, and are critting the PCs like crazy, it's okay to let up on the heroes a bit. Perhaps some of the enemies leave to inform others of the intruders. Or a leader takes a round off to verbally rub the PCs' ineptness in their faces. Or you can be more subtle, and have the enemies make less tactical decisions, spreading out attacks, or focusing on high-defense PCs. If you're the type to roll behind a screen, as a last resort you can fudge die rolls, turning crits into hits, or hits into misses. Be careful, however, about doing so too quickly. Battles in *13th Age* tend to start out with the enemies having the advantage and making things look dire, before the PCs pull out a daily power or take advantage of a high escalation die and suddenly change things around. If the escalation die is 2+ and you've got half the party unconscious or nearly there already, the players probably need a little help. One note on doing this, however; it's important to know your group. Some players will absolutely hate any GM help for bad rolls, and are willing to accept death as a penalty for their dice failures. Play it the way your group likes.

On the other side of the coin, if the players are rolling great and putting down the enemies left and right, consider upping the ante. We say this with a caveat, however. Sometimes it's good for the PCs to make it look easy and come away with a puffball fight. The players feel good and know they're badasses, and you can always throw a double-strength battle at them next time. The time to step in, however, is when you did want a tough battle, especially for a dramatic story reason, and not doing so means a boring fight for the players that will waste the next thirty minutes of game time. When this starts to happen, we suggest first adding more enemies, extra numbers of the type of creatures the PCs are already facing. Or introduce a sudden terrain effect that makes life a little more difficult for the heroes. If that's not working and you're using a GM screen, fudge misses into hits, and hits into crits only as a last resort, but try not to pick on any one player. In fact, at that point, it might be better to have all the enemies flee and you use up one of the PCs' icon advantages, suggesting the power of that icon was too much for the foes. Then you and the players can spin a tale about why they were so effective.

Overpowered/Underpowered Battles

If you throw your PCs into a battle you expected to be fun and challenging, only to quickly realize you went overboard and that triple-strength baddie that's three levels higher than the PCs is dropping one of them per round, for example, then you might want to make some adjustments. For most players, having natural attack rolls of 11–14 that don't hit (until the escalation die bumps up) isn't fun, if not downright frustrating, so keep an eye out. That's not to say occasionally throwing a much-higher-level enemy at them that's hard to hit doesn't work sometimes, but you should know why you're doing it going in and have options to help the PCs, such as having enemies relent to talk from a position of strength.

When you realize you've pitted the PCs against enemies or a situation that's just too much, pull it back some. Drop a really tough monster's defenses by a few points, or reduce its hit points by 10%, racking it up to terrain, an icon advantage, or whatever (or don't even tell the players what you're doing). Or use one of the options in the dice rolling examples above, such as having some enemies leave to report, or taunt the PCs instead of attacking. You shouldn't punish the players because you overestimated their capabilities.

On the other hand, if you build what you think is a good battle, only to get into it and realize that the monsters are less effective than expected, or forgot the wizard's *fireball* would basically remove all the mooks, leaving only a few squishy casters, go ahead and make the battle tougher. Increase the monsters' hit points by 10%, up their defenses by a point or two, bring in extra mooks (always a good option that won't overbalance things the other way), or even add a second wrecker that walks in behind the PCs just as they're celebrating their prowess. Be careful, however, with adjusting a battle stronger if the reason the PCs are doing so well is due to an icon advantage used before the fight, or some other smart ploy by the players to give their group an advantage. In those cases, reward the players' effort and creativity by letting them have the easy battle, and file it away so that next time, you can challenge them with a stronger battle that will get their attention.

Let's Talk, Not Fight

One last comment on battle adjustments. There may be times when you've designed a battle for the players, and then they decide to talk to their enemies, or sneak past them, or somehow avoid the fight while still pursuing their goals. Resist the urge to force the fight just because you spent time designing such a wonderful battle. If the players want to talk their way past the enemies, let them try (sometimes it will work, sometimes not). While battles are always one option for moving the story forward, they're often just dramatic sidenotes to the real story the PCs are pursuing, so don't get too attached. You can always save those monster stats and your well-designed battle for another time, changing fluff and other descriptions to fit the next battle, and the players will never know the difference. No need to waste work.

GM Battle Strategies

So you're building a battle and want to make it special. Or you've built what you think is a memorable battle, and want it to really have an impact on the players. What will set it apart? Here are a few more strategies you can use to improve the experience.

Unexpected Enemies

A classic strategy for experienced GMs is to hold back some enemies in a battle, only to introduce them a round or three later at a dramatic moment. This tactic works especially well in *13th Age* games thanks to the icon connections and relationship rolls of 5 that bring a complication with an advantage. Using that complication to introduce servants or enemies of the icon that wish the PCs harm after a battle against other enemies has started is always an option, and if the battle becomes harder due to it, well that's what comes from making powerful enemies.

A different method for using unexpected enemies comes into play when the players are a bit too familiar with the core monster stats. Present enemies that everyone thinks they know, such as a band of gnolls ("don't let them gang up on you with their *pack ferocity*"), but instead give the gnolls abilities from another type of monster that make them act differently. For example, the gnolls broke into a Lich King crypt and contracted ghoul fever. Now they fight individually and use claws instead of weapons, but their touch paralyzes enemies. The players won't be expecting that.

Vary the Strength and Occurrence of Battles

In the section on choosing the difficulty of a battle we talk about building standard, double-strength, or even triple-strength battles. It's also important to vary the sequence of when the PCs face those battles. Don't let the players get into the pattern of always saving their most powerful attacks and powers for the last battle before a full heal-up. Sure, sometimes it'll be four standard battles in a row, or two standard battles and then a double-strength fight right before the heal-up. But there's nothing wrong with throwing that double-strength battle at them first thing after a full heal-up, or as the second battle of the day. Let the story dictate the action and enemies, and make the players use their resources accordingly.

Another way to challenge the players and make them stretch their creativity is to sometimes make them wait an extra battle (or even two) before getting a full heal-up. You don't have to stick to a schedule on your full heal-ups. Maybe one of their early battles took few resources, so you decide they need to fight a fifth battle before they recover their resources. Or the players get to the "final" fight of the day, and use all of their best tricks to put the enemies down, making the battle easy. While they're still smiling but out of dailies, with only a recovery or two left each, hit them with another standard battle and see how creative they can be to win out without their best resources. You shouldn't do that every time, but using this tactic occasionally will make the players think twice about going nova with their best powers when things are dire.

Adding an extra standard battle is also a good option as a complication (a 5) from the use of an icon advantage, or maybe multiple complications adding up to an unexpected fight.

Recurring Villains

Don't be afraid to allow a particularly nasty, dangerous, tough, or fun villain to escape from the PCs, especially if it's an intelligent creature. In general, players like to win out and not leave loose ends, so when an enemy escapes they'll want to correct that mistake. It's good to give them a chance, whether it comes in the next battle, or when they meet that enemy again in a level or three. In fact, revisiting past failures is a great way to help the players feel like they're advancing in capability while also making the game world more vibrant.

One particularly useful tactic is to let a scheming but not overly powerful enemy escape that the PCs particularly dislike for whatever reason. Then have that enemy seek vengeance on the PCs, at first sending other foes against the heroes (but letting them know who was behind the attack), or even showing up with an ambush, only to slip away again. The key, however, is to let the

I like it when special villains get away. I handle the possibility at least two different ways.

Possible escape: *I make it clear that the villain is trying to escape, usually when the PCs are mostly engaged with other enemies or busy bleeding. I give the PCs a chance to break away and make an effort to stop the villain when there is something else they would rather be doing or when it's no sure thing they'll be able to stop the escape. If the villain manages to escape, the PCs know they had a chance to prevent it. If the PCs prevent the escape (and in my usual group they nearly always do!) they feel extra-pumped. They stopped me from getting a recurring villain. Victory!*

Fleeing for monsters: *When I've got an NPC or monster who feels like they should definitely become a recurring villain, I might arrange to have them flee the way PCs flee—guaranteed escape for one boss only, minions and champions left behind to their fates. When the PCs flee, they take a campaign loss. So when I let a villain just-get-away, fleeing style, I give the bad guys a campaign loss. That's usually the same thing as a campaign win for the PCs, though there might be subtle differences if the villains have significant enemies other than the PCs.*

There might be another option for handling a traitorous NPC. The thing that breaks your players' trust is that you lied to them. The campaign world depends on interesting interactions with NPCs and a really nasty traitor hits players in their game-buttons: "Hey! These interactions can screw us!"

So consider the path of truth. You could tell the players from the start: "Look, this NPC may not be right. There's a 50/50 chance they're going to betray you all. But your characters don't know that. And the better you roleplay not knowing that this NPC might betray you, the more I'm going to increase the chance that they won't betray you! But if you act all weird to this NPC, which I'll remind you that your characters have no reason to do, yet, then I'll make things worse for you. Oh yes."

Some groups will relish the chance to play with foreshadowing and dramatic beats. If they play so well they significantly alter the potential traitor's probabilities and win out, rewards should be significant.

PCs finish what they started, even if it takes a tier of adventuring, or perhaps a campaign, to get the chance. When they win out over the hated villain, most likely in a deadly battle that completes some storyline, the victory will be so much sweeter.

Using NPCs

To change the dynamic of a battle, have one or more NPCs join the group for a time. Perhaps they are combatants gained due to icon advantages and can help make a tough battle easier (we usually give such NPCs simple stats and have different players roll for their attacks). Or maybe an NPC needs protection, and the heroes must worry about keeping them safe instead of worrying about themselves. Don't use this tactic too often, especially with NPC combatant allies, since it will slow down battles, and be careful with turning the NPC into the star of the show instead of the PCs. (See page 240–249 in *13 True Ways* for more on running NPCs like this.)

Occasionally, you'll want to plant a traitor NPC with the heroes. It's an effective tactic, but one you probably won't be able to use more than once or twice, since the players won't ever trust any NPCs with them again. Of course, you can always have the servants of an icon demand that the PCs take someone with them and force the issue, but a better way is to start with helpful NPCs that assist the group. For the first few times that a NPC is among the PCs, have them provide useful knowledge, lend combat prowess, give out healing, or provide other benefits. Get the players used to helpful NPCs. Then when you introduce a traitor, it can have real impact, especially if the traitor was an NPC who was helpful to them over the course of many game sessions or levels of play. It also brings up the question of why did that NPC turn on them? Probably powerful leverage from an icon . . . which spawns more stories.

Running the Monsters

When the players have strong feelings about their enemies, it makes dispatching those enemies more satisfying. Give your enemies disgusting habits like spitting on the PCs, using vulgar insults, giving the PCs horrible nicknames, and similar measures to really get to the players. Also remember to keep the enemies talking, especially bosses, with quips and barbs as free actions during their turn or in response to things the PCs say. It helps make those enemies seem like more than the bag of hit points that they are. Too many times we've seen games where some villain is depicted via roleplaying very well before a fight breaks out, then the GM doesn't have the baddie say another word for the rest of the battle as they simply call out attack rolls and damage. It's a disservice to the monsters. Keep them talking, insulting the PCs and possibly revealing information useful to the heroes as they get worked up. Your players will enjoy putting down such foes even more, and the few seconds it adds to that monster's attack each round is worth it. Try to avoid the evil genius monologue, however, unless you're playing it for laughs.

Along with a running commentary, another way to make battles more memorable is to try to describe the action as much as possible. Each player generally has a picture in their head of what the battle looks like, and their PC's role in it. But it's harder to imagine the scene when all the GM gives you is, "The orc attacks with an axe. Does an 18 hit your AC?" You don't have to go into lengthy description to add value to a scene, but some adjectives and a sentence or two goes a long ways as you make your attack roll: "The bloody orc warrior leaps atop the table and delivers a mighty two-handed swing toward your head." And after you roll the attack and determine if it's a hit or not, continue with the description, in this case a miss: "You move sideways and the move throws off the orc's balance, causing it to miss you by inches." Even better is when you get the players to take over the description at that point, telling you what it looks like when the orc misses. After all, the game is a shared story.

Along the same lines, encourage your players to describe their attacks with a sentence or two. It will help you (or the player) describe what happens when their attack hits or misses. Some tables would rather not use the time for this description, which is their choice, but at the very least we suggest always letting a player describe a killing blow against a non-mook enemy (and perhaps even more fun, any attacks that drop multiple mooks). A player will remember the time they killed Thogg the Lesser by slicing the ropes holding a vat of dwarven ale that crushed him (and the jokes that came with it), representing their successful longsword attack far longer than they will remember killing an ogre with a longsword attack that did 13 damage.

Everyone Likes to Laugh

Roleplaying is supposed to be fun, and jokes around the table are usually a big part of what playing is all about. From time to time, include enemies and battle situations that have humorous elements on purpose. Give the players a little material and we guarantee they'll stretch it as far as it can go. Breaking up the dramatic tension is always good too, giving the game peaks and valleys and adding impact to each. Buffoonish antics, silly accents, slapstick, funny names, monsters trash-talking the PCs when they miss, monsters being surprisingly sympathetic to PCs who are having hopeless bad luck, monsters who hate other monsters in the fight who thank the PCs for killing the guy they hate, monsters falling into pits and trying to ransom themselves out with information on other monsters, and similar tactics can all lighten the mood and bring laughter.

Be Careful With Complex Monsters

Depending on your skill, enjoyment of complexity, and familiarity with the system, be careful building battles with too many complex monsters. By complex, we mean monsters with multiple abilities or multiple ability triggers. As a GM, you have plenty to think about while running a battle, and if there's too much complexity to the monsters, there's a good chance you'll miss things or forget about things, even with *13th Age's* simple natural roll triggers. That's usually not a big deal, and most of the time the players won't even know it, but it's less fun for a GM if at the end of a battle you really thought would challenge the players, it was a cakewalk for the PCs because you forgot the key mechanic to the main villain when the escalation die is even.

Two monsters that immediately come to mind as examples of complexity are the ogre mage knight in the *Bestiary*, and the half-orc legionnaire in the core book. Include more than one mage knight in a fight and you're tracking multiple attacks, multiple triggers, and multiple abilities each time. The legionnaire is less difficult, but every attack has multiple triggers, and if you have a troop of four or five of these monsters, you're trying to track a lot of bonuses and effects, and odds are you'll forget some of them. In general, most *13th Age* monsters are designed to be simple to run, leaving more time for description and story, but some are complex, so be aware of what you're getting yourself into.

Examples of Building Battles

Here are a couple of sample battles with notes on how we constructed them to show the use of theme, difficulty, terrain, and monster selection.

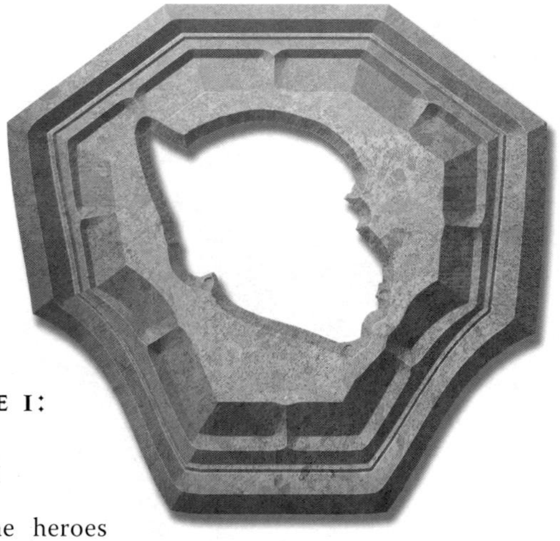

Example 1: Goblin Ambush

Theme: The heroes are seeking the entrance to an old mine said to hold some lost relic one of them seeks. One of the PCs has a 2-point conflicted relationship with the Orc Lord and rolled a pair of 5s at the end of the last session, so the GM decides that the character learns where the mine is located from a shady contact who gives the location, but also informs some goblin allies of their arrival; the contact will get a cut of whatever the goblins take. The theme is a goblin ambush (Orc Lord) in the hills leading to the mine.

Difficulty: There are five 2nd level PCs, and the GM decides that it will be slightly harder than a standard battle since the goblins know the PCs are coming. In this case, the GM decides to use monsters equivalent to six PCs instead of five (one more than standard). There's a decent chance of a surprise round too, so that will give the goblins a little more of an advantage.

Terrain: Rather than just having the goblins attack along the path to the mine, the GM decides to place the battle at an abandoned outdoor mining camp near the entrance to the mines. This choice lets the GM add some terrain features to the battle that will be interesting, and also possibly create problems for the PCs. The GM includes a couple of small wooden shacks for the goblins to hide in and jump out of, three pit traps covered with boards that are now rotted and hidden by dirt (previously dug when the camp was active), and a pair of wheeled wooden mine carts that the goblins have turned into their "big trick" of having some mooks roll down a slope to slam into enemies. The carts are also a way to add a funny element to the battle by setting up bad consequences for the goblins should they fumble an attack, or if the PCs do something clever, with cart mooks slamming into other goblins or plummeting into a pit, for example.

Once the PCs enter the camp, if at least one of them doesn't make a DC 15 Wisdom check to notice the goblins, the ambush starts with two goblin scum arriving in a cart. The terrain adds interest, but the GM decides the pits aren't such an advantage that it will adjust the numbers for the battle since the goblins could end up falling into them too.

Enemies: The GM wants the boss to have some staying power and decides to use a higher-level enemy, so a bugbear schemer (level 3) named Forntam (1.5 of 6) leads this band. He will use his big crossbow from the top of a nearby rise while commanding the goblins to attack. Once he switches to the club, it will be good to have plenty of allies for that +2 attack bonus he gives allies when he gets a natural even attack roll.

A leader needs followers, and goblin grunts make sense here. They're only 1st level, so the GM adds four to the battle (.7 x 4 = 2.8 of 6), one hiding in each shack and two on the ridge next to Forntam to be interceptors for anyone coming for him. Those two will use shortbows until the PCs engage them, while the first two go with melee attacks as they rush out of the shacks. Also, the goblins need plenty of allies to make use of their extra club damage when they outnumber foes.

Therefore, the comedic element. The GM rounds out the battle with eight 1st level goblin scum mooks that will help out the grunts and slow down the PCs from reaching Forntam (normally 1st level mooks would be .15 of a monster, but for 2nd level PCs, the rules suggest bumping mooks up a level, so these scum will count as one-fifth of a full monster; 8 x .2 = 1.6). There are two in each of the carts up on the hill, with the other four hiding in the two shacks with the grunts. If the goblins surprise the PCs, two mooks in one cart will roll down the hill and attack to start the battle (or fail humorously). The GM decides to give them one slam attack for twice their club damage (one attack roll) if the cart hits a PC, plus the PC must roll a normal save with failure resulting in a fall into a pit.

Other Adjustments: Since the goblins are mostly weaker than the PCs, the GM knows this battle could be too easy if the goblins roll poorly in the first few rounds. So the GM has a contingency plan. When the escalation die reaches 3, if the goblins are getting routed, the GM has a 3rd level hunting drake (self-created; 1.5) statted up and ready to go. It will wander into the battle hungry and start attacking, perhaps ripping a scum to shreds when it first shows up. That should get the players' attention. If need be, any remaining scum will flee at that point.

Example 2: Giant, Wolf, and Wurm

Theme: The heroes have strong ties to the Elf Queen and based on their icon rolls at the end of the previous session, the GM knows that she is in play. Recently a village of elves on the southern edge of the Dire Wood near the frosty Giantwalks has had some trouble with a family of frost giants that has been attacking them. The elves ask PCs with Elf Queen relationships for help. The giants live in a hold on an ice plane plateau in the mountains nearby, and the PCs are going to take the fight to the aggressive frost giants. The theme of the battle is a vicious fight against a frost giant and "friends" on an ice plane.

Difficulty: There are four 5th level PCs. This is the first time the PCs will face giants, and the GM wants to leave an impression. Plus, the GM has a nasty surprise for the players, a frost-wurm that will enter the battle too, perhaps the result of a complication from an icon roll, or because it's time for a tough fight. So the GM decides that it will be a double-strength battle. Including the terrain adjustment (1, below), the fight needs monsters worth the equivalent of seven PCs.

Terrain: The PCs pick up the trail of a giant a few hours later and begin tracking it on the icy plane. The GM decides that the terrain will be a factor in this battle, and so the winds are picking up, making visibility beyond far away difficult. The footing will also be slippery, requiring the PCs to make DC 20 Dexterity checks during the battle to move more than a few feet or they slip and lose the rest of their movement (but no issues for the giant or wolf), so the GM decides to count the terrain as one monster of their level (1).

The battle starts when the giant's wolf senses the PCs approaching, and the two stop and wait in the whiteout conditions. Suddenly the PCs spot the giant, waiting to see who is following. Seeing only puny humanoids, the giant and wolf attack. Bad enough for the PCs, especially since movement on the ice is difficult, but then at some point in the second round, the frost-wurm bursts out of the ice and shrieks. In fact, that's so good that the GM considers reducing the escalation die by 1 at that moment while the players all look at each other in stunned silence. Good times.

Enemies: For this battle, all of the enemies are higher level than the PCs. The giant is the obvious boss of the enemies, and frost giants are tough by nature, so he should stick around a bit. The battle consists of one large 7th level frost giant (3), along with his pet, a large 6th level winter wolf (2). That's plenty nasty, but the PCs have one more surprise. A large 6th level frost-wurm (2) hidden under the ice will sense the movement above and emerge into the battle during the second round. The hot-blooded PCs will draw its attention over the giant.

Other adjustments: This fight is tough. If things aren't going well for the PCs, the GM can have the frost-wurm show up a round later, or even grab the body of a slain wolf or giant and flee once it's staggered.

Incorporating Terrain into Battles

As GMs, we've all seen it. We set the stage for a fight, describing in detail the location with the gaping chasm over here and the hanging ropes over there, the low wall or hedge that offers concealment close to the bad guys standing guard, or the pool of swirling silver liquid right there, with the stone ramp that would give a PC the perfect opportunity to run up it and knock the bad guy in just to see what happens. Then the battle starts, and everyone, monsters and PCs, all end up in the middle of the area slogging it out until one side wins. Sure, it works. But is that what being a hero is all about? Perhaps not.

Using interactive terrain in battles, especially weird or interesting terrain, can make your *13th Age* battles more fun for both you and your players. The great thing about including terrain that has some thought behind it is that the terrain can benefit both the GM and the PCs simultaneously, or at different points in a battle. Interesting terrain options should encourage your players' curiosity, and that usually makes a battle more dynamic (and thus more memorable). Everyone remembers the time that Rosco the halfling pulled the pin on the vat of molten iron and totally fried Golt, the ogre jailor. Not so much the time that Rosco stabbed the ogre jailor for 14 damage, killing it by 3 points.

Using terrain benefits the GM because it sets the scene, bringing life and flavor to the enemies and the world, and it often gives those enemies some sort of advantage at the start of a battle, or even all battle long. The goblins know about the thermal vents, so they use their shiftiness to lure their enemies into the area then use their *shifty* ability to run when they hear the telltale sounds of hot steam coming. The hobgoblin chieftain keeps a pair of archers in the balcony of the ruined audience hall accessed via simple wooden ladders those archers will attempt to kick over during the battle if anyone tries to get to them. His troops (mooks) delay the PCs while the archers pick them apart. In fact, the addition of different terrain types, and especially interactive terrain (things either the monsters or the PCs can use during a battle), can make two battles against the same types of enemies completely different for both the GM and the players.

Including interesting terrain in battles also benefits the PCs. In addition to keeping battle scenes from getting stale or feeling like "the same old fight against another squad of orcs," you're presenting opportunities and options for players who like to do more than just declare an attack and roll a d20. Players playing classes like the rogue, ranger, and monk will especially appreciate your efforts, since having terrain to interact with plays to many of their talents and powers (Swashbuckle, Leaf on Wind, and terrain stunt to name a few), while not having any terrain detracts from their options. But any class can benefit from having terrain to use or that the enemies have to account for.

Of course, when you include terrain that helps the monsters in some manner, know that the players will most likely figure out a way to turn the tables on the bad guys, using the terrain against them in the same way. For example, a group of goblins are on top of a short stone tower throwing flasks of burning oil down on the PCs, damaging them fairly heavily to start a battle. But then one or more of the PCs manages to climb the tower, kill or drive off the goblin hurlers, and discovers a bucket full of flasks just waiting to be thrown. And the rest of the goblin horde is on the far side of the tower, just waiting to be incinerated. But that's fine. In fact, it's what you should want—the players interacting with the world you present them. And if they get to dispatch some annoying monsters in a cool new way, it makes the game better overall for everyone involved.

What is Terrain?

As far as setting a scene for a battle is concerned, terrain is any sort of feature besides monsters you as GM add to a battle to help make it come alive. It's the tumbled pillar providing cover or giving access to a high point, the hidden pit (perhaps with a monster waiting below), the clinging thorns where characters get stuck, the chandelier just across from the balcony that would make a great swing, the hanging wooden cage with the captive in it, the frozen pool of purple ice glowing with magic, the unholy flame of purification burning in the center of the temple that can be manipulated, and the giant mirror in the wizard's laboratory that shows images of another place and crackles with teleportation magic, to name just a few possibilities.

Terrain also includes natural and environmental factors that can hinder the PCs or creates a challenge they must deal with to progress. For example, a room filled with poison gas that slowly drains recoveries from the PCs, a water-filled chamber where the PCs have to swim to move (and possibly drown), a muddy bog with deep holes or quicksand, or a lava chamber filled with molten rock and hot, poisonous gasses that deal fire and poison damage every round.

The important idea is that it's something the PCs can (or must) interact with as part of a battle to obtain their goal or defeat the enemy. Terrain challenges also occur outside of battle during exploration, of course, but we're talking about how to use it in battles.

The "Stand and Hack It Apart" Problem

So you've decided to liven up your battles with some terrain, fleshing out your scenes and giving your monsters and PCs something to interact with, but the players continue to move their characters into a tight wad in the middle of the field of battle and slog through a hackfest, even the ones who could benefit from using the terrain. How to break them of the habit and get them using the terrain more? Two good options are to let the monsters use the terrain to crush the PCs, and to reward PCs who do interact with the terrain and try new things, either with better-than-normal outcomes or at least with entertaining descriptions when those PCs fail.

When we say "crush" the PCs, we mean have the enemies the PCs are facing use the terrain in a creative and highly effective way that makes those enemies more deadly than they would be normally. And keep using it until the PCs make them stop. Eventually, the players should realize that the enemies are stronger than normal because they're using their surroundings to their advantage, so they need to adjust their tactics to negate or mitigate the advantage, or they'll continue to pay the cost in hit points, recoveries, and limited powers. Such an advantage could be the equivalent of having one more enemy in the battle, or so strong it turns the fight into a double-strength battle. Make sure to vary the difficulty imposed by different types of terrain when you include terrain that gives enemies a benefit.

For example, a bandit crime lord has a special Chamber of Initiation within his stronghold. When the PCs intrude, he sends all of the wannabe gang members (mooks) into the chamber to face the PCs, while he and his lieutenants watch from a high balcony. The crime lord has an extra trick for them all, too. He's rigged the chamber to have unstable footing, spikes that emerge from the walls and floor, and other dangers attacking everyone on the ground level, mooks included. If the PCs stay to fight the mooks, the terrain will take a heavy toll on them. They need to change tactics and get to the crime lord, or even better, find a way to get the crime lord down into the chamber with them, where he'll take damage from the terrain too.

When we talk about rewarding PCs who do show curiosity about your well-thought-out terrain choices, or who try risky things using that terrain, or come up with cunning plans involving the terrain, we mean *have them succeed or fail grandly*. When the PCs have a creative idea for using terrain, and their rolls support it, you should reward them with more than they expected from the attempt, especially if doing so poses a risk of personal injury to them. Make a success really cool. And if the attempt is replacing one of their normal attacks for their class, make sure a success comes with at least as much damage and/or other conditions applied to the enemies affected as one of their attacks would have generated, and preferably a bit more. You want the other players to see the PC pull it off, tell the player "that was cool," and then try to think up ways they could have a moment in the spotlight using the terrain.

Interacting with the terrain, or using it for some trick, won't always work out well for the PCs. Perhaps the monk tries to tip over the highest barrel of lantern oil in a stack to have it fall on those below, only to have the whole stack come loose under them, sending the monk down along with the barrels. Or the rogue's attempt to knock a bandit sentry off his perch as she leaps from a high tree branch to the tower platform where the man stands with his back turned ends with a long fall. So the PC fails, but such failures usually bring a round of laughs from the table for the attempt, and it's dramatic and memorable (and usually brought up as a fun memory for the next few sessions or even the rest of the campaign). While such failures can be bad for the PC or the group, try to avoid penalizing a player too much for the attempt, since you don't want your players to avoid future attempts because it cost them dearly. The exception to that, however, is when you outline exactly what the cost will be for a failure and give the player the option of continuing with their course of action. In that case, they knew what they were in for, including the possibility of death.

Also consider making close failures have the desired effect, but also include the negative consequence for the PC (failing forward). Using the examples above, the monk rides a barrel to the ground, where it explodes, sending lantern oil spraying on everyone in the room, allies included, but mostly on the enemy. Or the rogue gets one hand on the sentry's foot, pulling the man off the tower with her as they both fall, but he lands on top of her taking no damage (but at least he's not up on the tower anymore).

Using the Best Terrain for the Scene

Using the right terrain or environmental conditions for a battle is also a good way to set the scene for the players, especially if you don't use maps or miniatures for your games. Any extra details the players get in imagining the setting will help them visualize what's going on and also help them avoid the "I stand there and attack" problem, since they can indicate where they are in relation to some terrain element or how they use the terrain. Don't be afraid to be descriptive. The more description you give to an element, the more likely the players are to pick up on your emphasis and become interested in trying to interact with it. (Note, an evil GM will use this trick every so often to emphasis something unimportant while they give only passing mention to the terrain that's going to cause the PCs trouble.)

So what is the "best" terrain? Generally, it's whatever makes sense to you for the scene, and what will intrigue at least a few of the players. Are you fighting a mad wizard in his tower? Then magical effects like portals and walls of force, equipment like vats of acid and tall climbable bookshelves, and magical lighting that sparks and fades repeatedly might be appropriate. A goblin lair? Difficult footing only navigated by small creatures or those who know the path, refuse piles with sharp objects hidden by the junk, noise-maker tripwires, disgusting items like a big cauldron of elf-ear soup, guano-covered walls that hide goblins "painted" to look like the walls, and disease-infested vermin might be fitting. In general, the logic of your world should show through most of the time with terrain details. That way, if the PCs encounter similar terrain in the future, they will know what to expect, and how to negate it or use it to their advantage. A general consistency with their expectations also works for the GM, because every once in a while, you can insert a bit of terrain that is not normal for the scene or that acts differently than expected, and catch the players off guard. That can be rewarding too.

So what's more fun for the players? An empty, dry, roughly 20-foot by 20-foot cave in an underground lair that holds four nearby orc sentries and has one other tunnel exiting beyond them? Or a 30 x 70 cavern filled with strange fungus that grows up the left-hand wall, some of it glowing with an eerie, orange phosphorescence? The second cavern is damp and leaks small trails of orange-lit moisture across the floor. There's an overturned mine cart halfway between the PCs and four far away orc sentries, who stand next to the only other exit in the place.

The first description encourages the PCs to move up to the orcs and bash it out with them until one side wins. The second description might make the PCs wonder whether something in the fungus or water is dangerous (it could be), puts them far away so ranged attacks come into play, and, depending on initiative, gives one side or the other a chance to upright the cart and turn it into a ramming vehicle if they are bold enough to try it (the orcs will for sure), or use it as cover.

Classes and Terrain

Different classes will view terrain differently. Here's a quick rundown of each class and what terrain types may appeal to those playing them or might challenge the PC more than normal. It's always good to present terrain that both appeals to some members of the party, and limits others, all in the same battle.

Barbarian: Barbarians are all about having chances to show off how big and strong they are. Terrain that lets the barbarian PC push objects over on enemies, climb to reach enemies, or requires enduring pain or ignoring conditions to reach enemies is right up their alley. Terrain that requires careful study (Intelligence) or deep insights (Wisdom) to navigate, avoid, or understand will often be more troublesome for them, unless it plays to one of their backgrounds. They tend to leave the odd runes on the walls or the unnatural pools of purple goop to spellcasters and others interested in esoteric madness.

Bard: If there's a chance for flair, the bard is there, so any opportunity to swoop in and save the day (or a captive) works well for them, especially if it doesn't involve being in the front line. A bard probably won't be interested in pushing a dead tree over on the bandits, but she'll love to soothe the runaway horses on the carriage she's riding on top of before the team goes over a cliff. Some bards love the opportunity to play with magical effects; others will get as far away as possible. Most bards will leave terrain that involves self-harm or unnecessary risk without great reward to the fighter, rogue, or barbarian.

Chaos Mage: When it comes to terrain, a chaos mage lives in a special place. Half the time, the mage is creating the terrain effects that everyone else has to deal with. The weirder it is, the more the chaos mage likes it. Most chaos mages aren't very physical and will leave opportunities to interact with terrain that requires exertion to others. Similar to wizards and other spellcasters, magic terrain that requires Intelligence to overcome or manipulate is a favorite, as are any opportunities to use their force of personality (Charisma checks). A strange crystal fragment or ancient artifact that they can manipulate for random effects during a battle is probably about as good as it gets. Of course, with a chaos mage you're never quite sure what they'll try.

Cleric: Terrain that works for clerics depends on the cleric, of course. A cleric with the Strength domain might enjoy using terrain similar to a fighter, while one with the Healing domain might be more interested in manipulating the terrain to help the group succeed or making a Wisdom check to figure out how to use some piece of terrain and then instructing an ally on what to do with it. One area that most clerics excel at are rituals that manipulate the environment of the battle. If they can find a way to redirect the energies of ritual in progress in their allies' favor, all is well. One type of terrain that almost always gives them difficulty and they try to avoid, however, is anything involving Dexterity such as swinging on ropes, leaping chasms, or balancing on ledges to reach the bad guys. Clerics usually don't want to risk taking themselves out of a fight that way, since their healing is always vital to the rest of the party.

Commander: A commander treats terrain like another ally. Most commanders will try to gain as much information about the scene of a battle as possible while they assess the fight. Then they will direct their allies on how to take advantage of that terrain, suggesting choke points, high ground, or luring enemies into dangerous terrain. Commanders are hearty enough that feats of Strength and Dexterity are always an option, especially if they will help the commander get into a position to see all the combatants early in the fight. Terrain that enemies use against the PCs is simply an opportunity for the commander and their allies to turn the tables on those enemies, and most commanders take great pleasure in making it so. While commanders know how to take advantage of magical and environmental effects that damage or hinder, most tend to avoid interacting with other types of magical effects that require careful study and deep intellect since they're usually too busy watching their allies, except for the rare strategist, of course.

Druid: The ways that druids approach and use terrain are as varied as the types of druids. Warrior druids and shifter druids act much like fighters and barbarians, looking for opportunities to use their strength to good effect. Many shifter druids also like to climb, balance, and use terrain to avoid or hinder enemies, depending on what form they take. Those with a caster bent are especially adept at handling magical and environmental terrain, especially the types they are specialized in or that involve elemental damage of some sort. They will often find ways to shape it from one thing into something else that serves their need. The terrain that gives druids trouble or they find less interesting depends on where their talents lay, but anything that tests their Constitution or that reeks too much of civilization can be troublesome.

Fighter: Much like the barbarian, fighters look for opportunities to use their Strength and hardiness, and sometimes their Dexterity. They're also good at using terrain for personal tactics, such as placing themselves in a position where enemies must come through them to reach the fighter's allies, forcing those enemies to consider passing through deadly or hindering terrain. They relish chances to use their maneuvers to knock enemies off precarious positions, to draw an enemy into terrain that is harmful to both and outlast the foe, or to use terrain to position themselves among many enemies, locking them down in melee, such as leaping off a wall into the center of a horde of mooks. Being action-focused, most fighters don't do well when interacting with terrain that requires complex setup to achieve a dicey move, that involves objects or energies they consider "dangerously magical," or that risks them losing their maneuverability. In fact, pits, webs, and other terrain that can get a fighter stuck are perhaps more effective against them than terrain that deals damage.

Necromancer: Necromancers usually excel at interacting with terrain that involves study and Intelligence, or requires the manipulation of magical effects. Strange substances and anything to do with death also pique their curiosity. Much like wizards, necromancers tend to avoid terrain that is harmful or that requires great Strength or Dexterity or especially hardiness, unless it also involves dead things, of course. Necromancers with skeletal minions and other summoned undead have no issue sending such creatures into damaging terrain to clear the path, to test the terrain, or to surprise enemies using the terrain who believe themselves safe from any "sane" foes who would avoid the harmful effects of that terrain.

Monk: Each type of different terrain is simply a new opportunity for a monk to test themselves on the obstacle course of life, as well as offering options for describing their attack sequences. Terrain that requires Strength or Dexterity to navigate or manipulate appeals the most. Other terrain that requires deep insight into its true nature to avoid harm or that the monk can use to improve attacks or defenses is also an opportunity for them to shine. Monks that have the Leaf on the Wind talent are looking for opportunities to climb and balance high above the ground, and should find them often. Terrain that acts as an impediment to movement is also ripe for exploitation, since many of the forms monks use include the ability to fly or leap great distances, though that can lead to a monk getting isolated from allies. While many monks are skilled at dealing with physical terrain, most aren't showboats (though a few are) and they'll leave the daring rescues and improbable use of terrain to harm their enemies to the bards and rogues and barbarians, instead relying on their own fighting skills to solve an issue once they use the terrain to get into a superior striking position. Terrain that can slow them down through magical effects that require Intelligence or force of personality situations that require Charisma can be a problem, however, and they tend to avoid interacting with terrain that is obviously arcane and magical in nature, leaving it to the spellcasting types unless they have some background with such matters. (*Editor's note*: This isn't worth a full **RobSays** sidebar, but suffice to say that monks in the campaigns I run almost always seem to be showboats competing with everyone else to do the coolest things. The Improbable Stunt talent lends itself to this worldview!)

Occultist: The occultist sees the world differently, and sometimes reality adapts around them, so what seems like a terrain obstacle to most is nothing to them. In fact, the occultist will often warp the surrounding terrain to suit their needs when facing enemies, even if for only a moment. For that reason, it's good to give a player playing the occultist a full allotment of terrain options to incorporate into their attack descriptions, if that's how they roll. Magical terrain and terrain that requires intuition and intellect to manipulate or negate is their bread and butter. Although each iteration of the occultist is different, most of the time their physical skills trail their mental ones, so you won't see the occultist going out of their way to make daring leaps, slide down banners, or hold a door or gate shut against enemies. They leave that to others. Because of the delayed time that often affects them and with it delayed healing, the occultist tends to avoid terrain that poses direct harm, otherwise they could get into deep trouble before aid takes hold.

Paladin: Much like the fighter, a paladin looks for personal opportunities to use the local terrain to their advantage. For them, nothing beats holding the charge of the enemy as they fight at the top of a set of stairs or other superior position, keeping the enemies off their comrades. For paladins that can challenge enemies, they can force foes to face them in a dangerous area or suffer penalties. True, the paladin might be harmed by the terrain as well, but they can take it, whereas most of their foes are unwilling to do so. Paladins with more of a leadership bent will often identify advantageous terrain options and then direct their allies on how to use those advantages so as to draw the most dangerous enemy to the paladin. Terrain that most paladins will avoid is anything that forces them to balance or hold on precariously using Dexterity, since they can't gloriously defend their friends while worrying about falling. Most paladins are also straightforward about defeating their enemies with courage and honor, rather than "playing tricks" on foes using terrain that doesn't involve superior positioning.

Ranger: Rangers have a knack for using the terrain around them to good advantage. Perhaps it comes from often having to deal with enemies while alone in the wilds. Their skill in leveraging natural terrain is unmatched, especially for ranger trackers with the terrain stunt power. Given a few terrain options (and you always should give them options in rural or wilderness settings), they will figure out creative ways to quickly put enemies at a disadvantage. They also like to take on terrain challenges that involve Strength or Dexterity to put themselves in a superior position to use their melee or ranged attacks, bringing destruction to their enemies in the most efficient way possible. Rangers tend to avoid terrain effects created by magic alone, unless they have experience with the Elf Queen or a religious background. Likewise, urban terrain or non-natural terrain that requires careful study (Wisdom) or expert knowledge (Intelligence) is best left to allies skilled in such things since it often ends up just confusing them.

Rogue: Rogues look for every advantage they can find to put their enemies down quickly and avoid harm to themselves. To their mind, battlefield terrain always holds such advantages for those willing to risk it. And that suits a rogue just fine. Leaps, tumbles, and amazing feats of dexterity are all part of the rogue's expertise, and most will attempt to manipulate the local terrain using Strength if it involves climbing or even bringing the hurt to a group of enemies by timing something just right. Rogues with the Swashbuckle talent must have plenty of terrain to work with, always. Giving them a blank palette is a disservice, and it limits the rogue player's fun. Every swashbuckler should have at least one thing they can jump off of, leap over, swing from, or otherwise manipulate to make themselves look awesome each battle, and a slew of options is even better. Like most of the other physical classes, terrain that involves study or obscure knowledge won't be as interesting to them, unless of course it's also linked to some sort of trap or gives them a chance to acquire great wealth. Some magical terrain effects might stymie a rogue, though most players will devise a cunning plan to use such terrain to their advantage if they can just pull "something" off. When a rogue's player is talking like that, you're doing your job with terrain.

Sorcerer: Like the chaos mage, sorcerer players look for terrain that can insert some randomness into a battle. If it's magical terrain they can manipulate, so much the better. While most sorcerers shy away from interacting with terrain that involves feats of strength, a few might be willing to use their quickness in the right situation, or test their pain endurance in the case of those with high Constitution. But like the cleric with their domains, almost any terrain challenge could be of interest to a sorcerer depending on their heritage talents. A sorcerer with the Undead Remnant heritage, for example, will be a sucker for that wall of zombie parts emitting negative energy that can be manipulated to send out bursts of death magic. Although most sorcerers are willing to test their luck when terrain options are available, few choose to involve themselves with terrain obstacles or opportunities involving or created by divine magic.

Wizard: Being one of the more cerebral classes, most wizards know well enough to let their allies make great leaps across chasms, raise portcullises with brute strength, and pull off fancy physical maneuvers. They have magic, after all, and there are plenty of cantrips or utility spells or rituals that can fill in quite nicely to create or manipulate terrain effects to the benefit of their allies. Why climb the wall to access the gatehouse when some *ghost voices* and a few *light* tricks will bring the enemy out of the gate? Wizards are also good at understanding and manipulating magical terrain, and most know a little of this or that about all sorts of topics, which could provide information that saves them and their allies a lot of trouble and pain ("Yes, that fungus is poisonous, and yes it will incapacitate you if you move through it . . . unless you soak a rag in wine and breathe through it, in which case you'll grow pain resistant for a time."). One other thing their great intellects do for wizards is that they'll often devise cunning uses of terrain, if given enough time to think about how to use it. Unfortunately, most battles don't offer such luxury unless the wizard and their allies get the drop on the enemies, but if there's a way to use a spell on some piece of terrain to create even more havoc among the enemy, a wizard will figure it out very quickly and put that knowledge to good use.

The Mechanics of Using Terrain

The *13th Age* core rules don't delve too deeply into terrain and its usage, preferring to keep things simple for the GM and the players. But that doesn't mean a GM shouldn't provide terrain options to players both during battles and during exploration. Adding detail without adding complex mechanics enhances player immersion. You may have seen various uses of terrain effects in published adventures or other works, but here are some mechanical details on how to use terrain during battles. Of course, you should use it as little or as much as your group prefers.

The core rulebook suggests that a terrain advantage should give the group with the advantage a +2 attack bonus in general and leaves it at that (page 187). The bonus is fine, but as always, how you apply it should depend on the situation. If the PCs or their enemies are using terrain to ambush an enemy group, for example, the attack bonus makes sense. But if someone is instead using it to improve their defensive position or make it harder for enemies to attack them? There's no reason you couldn't give them a +2 bonus to AC or PD instead (or maybe even MD if the terrain provides a magical or mental assist). Or maybe the bonus could apply to skill checks (or to saves for monsters, which can act like a skill check). Also, if a PC has a great idea or does a great job (high roll on a skill check) manipulating the terrain, feel free to increase the bonus as you see fit.

For example, during a battle against drow in a temple chamber whose floor is made of stained glass, the drow know that the purple panes are safe to move on and others will break, sending the person through the jagged glass. When any creature moves in the chamber, it must succeed on an easy save or take damage and get stuck. Knowing the right color lets the drow have a better chance of moving safely (they move like they're dancing), and they gain a +2 bonus to their saves, or +4, since this a specialized situation that's not about monster vs. PC d20 rolls. Eventually, the PCs can gain the bonus too once they figure out the proper color.

Our GM screen lists the skill check chart (it's also on page 186 of the core rulebook), giving the DCs for tier and impromptu damage amounts. This should be your guide when the PCs interact with terrain to seek an advantage (or how much damage to deal when their attempt fails). When a PC decides to use terrain during battle, and there's some element of risk to it, let them make an appropriate skill check using a DC based on the difficulty you assign. If they succeed, they achieve what they were trying to do, or you can give them the +2 bonus (to attack, defenses, saves, or skill checks as appropriate), as long as the player gives you a good narration of what their character did. If they fail, assign impromptu damage if it applies, or some other failure condition. Remember the fail forward approach too, if it makes sense; perhaps they succeed, but in a way they weren't expecting that causes problems, or they outright fail, but failure opens up new options.

For example, a goblin shaman traps the PCs in a room with a handful of goblin warriors and her bodyguards are pouring vats of acid into the room. A PC wants to climb some stairs and then try to leap to the top of a wall where a winch will open the door out. The GM calls it a tough jump as a move action and assigns a DC of 20 using Strength and their Mad Leaper background. The player gets a final result of 18 and the PC comes up short, sliding down the wall. But it was close enough that the GM rules they happen to land on a mantel stone that causes a secret door to open. Great, right? They found a different exit. Except that there's a zombie orc in the opening, and it now joins the battle. The failure leads to a new twist.

You shouldn't worry about skills checks for simple actions that are purely meant for flavor like a PC wanting to leap on a table to get eye-to-eye with a giant before an attack. Save skill checks involving terrain for actions that are truly advantageous or that have a penalty for failure. It helps if you make a note on what you think the DC should be to interact with a terrain element ahead of time, next to that element's description, such as [DC 15 Str check to jump it; 2d6 damage on a fall]. That way when

a PC chooses to do so, you're ready, and you can always adjust the DC up or down on the fly based on what they're trying to do.

Use the normal DC most of the time for actions using terrain that gives the PC or their allies a slight advantage in some way. The more the players know that if they try something exciting or weird, they have a good chance of pulling it off, the better. For monsters, make it an easy save (6+). For example, a rogue wants to jump to a chandelier from a table, swing over the thugs in front, and land next to the bad guys' leader to make an attack without being intercepted. Or a wizard attempts to decipher the runes on a magical obelisk that will empower her spells, adding one extra damage die to them during the battle (perhaps even her suggestion to the GM).

Use the hard DC when a PC attempts to use the terrain for a big advantage for them personally or for one of their allies, especially if it lasts more than a round, or that helps the entire group for a short time. On the monster side, it's a normal save (11+). For example, the barbarian tries to leap off a balcony grabbing the top of a banner attached there, enveloping two hobgoblins below in the heavy tapestry and making them stuck (easy save ends) so he can go fight the squishy battle caster. Or the paladin slams the door to the armory and tries to hold it against a pair of charging bugbears, buying his allies a full round to heal.

Use the ridiculously hard DC when a PC attempts to use the terrain in some amazing way that might seriously damage enemies, that removes the PC or an ally from danger for a round or three, that gives their allies an advantage for longer than one round, or that provides a similar strong advantage. Usually, failure also has a strong negative consequence, whether damage, a condition applied, or making the situation worse than it was before (but still failing forward). For monsters, it's a hard save (16+). For example, a sorcerer calls on his infernal heritage and attempts to redirect the semi-sentient Hellish vapors seeping out of a demon statue to envelop a group of sahuagin on high ground, causing damage to all of them. Failure means the vapors envelop him, and possibly the other PCs immediately. Or a fighter attempts to lift a heavy stone gate singlehandedly, which will allow a rival group of kobolds to attack the goblins that the PCs are fighting, making the battle a cakewalk. Failure means the fighter gets stuck and vulnerable, partially trapped under the door (save ends).

A Note on Using Heights and Enemies that Fly

While there are class options for players who want to be good at ranged attacks, many groups may be light in that area as a team. If that's the case with your group, understand that if you use ranged enemies against them, especially ones that are hard to reach due to high terrain or because they can fly, those enemies will have a big advantage. You might want to limit your use of such terrain or enemies with those movement capabilities to only when you want to challenge the PCs and remind them of their weakness against ranged opponents.

In our games, we believe a height advantage due to terrain is fine, as long as the PCs can reach those enemies with realistic skill checks (and then possibly gain the same advantage against remaining foes). We're less inclined to let enemies fly and make ranged attacks at the same time, since that slows down battles and makes the enemies tougher as well, unless, of course, it's for an exceptional enemy (like a dragon outdoors).

Terrain and Environments

The *13th Age* system has three tiers, or environments, built into it to help GMs in creating and describing locations and scenes for adventure: adventure tier, champion tier, and epic tier. These tiers can also be helpful in presenting appropriate terrain options.

While there's plenty of "normal" terrain that the PCs will interact with in any tier—walls to climb, chasms to cross, puzzle doors to examine, shrub hedges to navigate, and more—in general, you want to up the ante on the terrain options you present as the PCs climb in tiers. Champion-tier environments should be more extreme and fantastic than those in adventurer tier, and epic tier more so than champion tier.

For example, in adventurer tier, the heroes must descend into a shallow cave system inhabited by kobolds serving the Three that's filled with their traps. In champion tier, they are instead heading into a quicksand-infested underground swamp in the upper underworld that's filled with leveled-up lizardmen who are part of a snake cult dedicated to the Black. In epic tier, those heroes might be in the deep underworld and must enter a living dungeon linked to the Red and shaped like a giant egg rising from the depths. It's filled with recently hatched wyrmspawn humanoids, and the very walls of the place are infused with ancient dragon magic that isn't happy about the PCs being inside.

One of the best ways to use terrain to distinguish the different environments is through magical effects. The standard assumption for the *13th Age* system, and the Dragon Empire setting, is high magic. But that doesn't have to mean that magic is everywhere the PCs go. You could use a lot of nonmagical terrain early on during the adventurer tier, only hinting at the stronger magical terrain effects in stories the heroes hear about, or maybe if they accidentally wander into a higher-tier environment, especially something connected to one of the icons. For example, the PCs are in a village of halfling folk being troubled by goblins and their nasty pranks, but just up the path are the ruins of an ancient dwarven city. No one goes there because of the stone golems guarding the broken gates. If the PCs choose to investigate, they see a pair of stone golems squash a squad of goblins with ease. Continuing forward will be at their peril.

By the time the PCs are in champion tier, they'll start to discover some of the wonders of the world, and encounter powerful enemy spellcasters and ritualists who can generate deadly terrain, not to mention facing more deadly iconic servants and terrain effects. In some of the places they travel, magic will be commonplace, perhaps used in place of some technology, or used to protect communities in some way. The elven village in the Wild Wood, for example, is smack in the middle of the lands of the Blackrun werewolves, but the druidic magic infusing the village's moon stones keeps them out, until it starts to fail, of course. The PCs will have to try to restore the stones as the werewolves attack.

Once the PCs have arrived in epic tier, let the magic and fantastical elements fly. Their lives should be made both easier and more difficult by the magic that seems to be everywhere they go. Why walk or ride horses when you now have access to flying carpets and airships? Of course, epic magic now means epic terrain and environments, especially locations in the overworld and underworld. Perhaps a Diabolist cult has found a ritual to open a hellhole wherever they want, and they choose one of the Seven Cities. Now that metropolis has been overrun with lesser demons as the cult is finishing the final parts of the ritual to fully unleash the hellhole. Not only do the PCs need to stop the cultists, but now in addition to facing demons and other unholy enemies, the very walls of the metropolis try to consume them, and horrible and disgusting magical effects are everywhere.

Even if you prefer using a low-magic setting, you can still use terrain to set off the different tiers. It may be places the PCs find from the old days—architectural or technological wonders they've never seen, for example. Or maybe you simply up the danger ante: short falls off a rope bridge that will only hurt a PC in adventurer tier become long falls into a mist-filled gorge that probably still won't kill the PC, but the monsters down there will in champion tier. And a fall in epic tier might just be to the death, if a PC decides to push their luck.

Example Terrain Across Environments

Here are some more examples of similar terrain across environments to give you a sense of how to ramp up your use of terrain by tier. Of course, any of these could happen at a different tier than shown depending on the individual game.

Example 1

Adventurer tier: A stone door with a gargoyle bust carved into it blocks the way. The PCs must find the hidden catch in the carving to open it (a skill check). Failure means a pull rope rings a bell, bringing the enemies beyond, and perhaps a mechanical trap makes the gargoyle bite the PC with their hand in the mouth.

Champion tier: Instead of a mechanical catch, the gargoyle face is animated and can speak and listen. It asks the PCs a riddle, and if they answer correctly, they may pass. If the player doesn't know the answer, a PC skill check could suffice. Failure means the gargoyle construct summons an earth elemental to deal with intruders.

Epic tier: The gargoyle face is animated, but it also has three different colored gems inset within eight-inch-deep holes in the door. The gargoyle talks to them and questions them, revealing some clue to opening the door unrelated to the gems, probably involving the utterance of the correct phrase. Then it tells the PCs they must choose the correct gem from the inset to open the door (lying to them). All three are trapped, each with a different effect. One forms stone around a hand inside, trapping the PC. Another infuses the PC with an elemental spirit. The last leaves a mark that is a curse of some sort.

Example 2

Adventurer tier: The PCs must cross a cavern filled with fungus and mushrooms. Moving safely requires an Intelligence skill check to notice which plants are dangerous, with failure resulting in mushrooms that disperse spores to disorient humanoids, making them vulnerable. Enemies immune to the spores wait at the far side of the cave.

Champion tier: The PCs must cross a cavern filled with fungus and mushrooms that glow with violet phosphorescence. It requires a skill check or two, and those who fail cause some of the mushrooms to release spores. The spores burrow into the PCs' flesh causing damage. Each PC must then roll a save, with failure indicating that the spores then emerge from the PC's flesh as a fungal-blood monster that now attacks.

Epic tier: The PCs must cross a cavern filled with fungus and mushrooms that glow with violet phosphorescence. The bodies of many humanoids lay entombed within the fungus, some skeletal and others still rotting. If anyone fails a skill check to carefully move through the place, they set off a spore cloud that sends all in the cave into a shared hallucinogenic dreamstate. They may end up fighting perceived enemies who are their allies, or simply have to escape from the dream by succeeding at a skill challenge, taking psychic damage for every round they remain.

Example 3

Adventurer tier: A local population center is under attack from undead. The locals grew lax with the sacrifices to the Lich King and divinations reveal that the ritual wards have failed or were broken. The PCs must restore the wards surrounding a statue of the Lich King at the center of the graveyard or crypt. The PCs must spread out to different points around the statue chamber and use skill checks to fix the wards using ritual wordings. Undead rise and attack, with more undead coming forth with each failure.

Champion tier: The PCs must restore the wards as above, but the graveyard or crypt is alive, animated by a dark spirit who wishes to remain free. It creates obstacles drawn from the old crypts and cairns to interrupt the PCs during their ritual, has undead or dead tree roots burst from the ground to try to pull the PCs down into the cold earth, and actively resists with negative energy feedback against PCs with each ritual skill check failure.

Epic tier: The graveyard or crypt is a major node of the Lich King's power. Not only are there powerful undead guarding it, but the memories of the dead interred within now invade the world as psychic projections. As the PCs navigate the warding ritual, they must make skill checks to avoid feeding these nightmares. When someone fails, the Lich King's projections surge out across the world, corrupting areas that hadn't previously been touched by his power. The PCs are going to have to track down each of the problems they've inadvertently created, unless future icon advantages indicate that some of them can be taken care of by other allies of their patrons.

HANDLING BACKGROUNDS

When working with players to develop their PC backgrounds, remember that in the *13th Age* RPG, backgrounds serve three main functions: character development, world building, and resolving skill checks.

As a character development tool, backgrounds are one of the ways players tell the GM what sort of adventures they want to have. A player whose ranger PC has the backgrounds "Mountain trapper," "Exiled child of the frost barbarian king," and "Served in the Dwarf King's army during the Ice Troll War" is probably looking to fight trolls and similar monsters, hang out with dwarves, and participate in (or try to stay out of) political intrigue.

As a world building tool, backgrounds help shift a significant portion of the GM's work to the opposite side of the table. By choosing those backgrounds, that player told the GM that ice trolls exist, and are a big enough problem that the Dwarf King raised an army to fight them; and that frost barbarians exist, are ruled by a king, and certain crimes warrant exile under their system of justice—even the child of the king is not immune.

As a mechanic for resolving skill checks, well-written backgrounds are useful in a variety of situations, and give the character's actions a larger context by tying into the setting and the icons. When the ranger is able to find shelter in a blizzard, impress a minor noble, and track a troll to its lair, it's not because they had Outdoor Survival, Diplomacy, and Tracking on their character sheet—it's because they have a backstory that's rooted in a specific place and time, that links them to the Dwarf King, and that has made them the adventurer they are today.

HELPING PLAYERS WRITE EFFECTIVE BACKGROUNDS

Sometimes, players create backgrounds for their characters that don't serve one or more of these purposes. Such backgrounds might have limited use as skills, fail to say anything about the world, or don't help the character stand out. The core book doesn't offer much guidance, providing generic sample backgrounds such as "animal trainer" and "soldier". (Don't tell Rob and Jonathan we said that, though.)

To help players get the most out of their backgrounds, we're suggesting a play strategy first offered by Philippe-Antoine Menard. Ask your players to create backgrounds that each include at least two of the following elements: a place, a historical event, an organization, or an icon.

Here are a few sample backgrounds created using this template:

- Escaped crew member of a pirate ship cursed by the **Diabolist** to sail the **Iron Sea** for eternity *(Icon, Place)*
- Organizer of the legendary **35th birthday celebration** for the **Emperor** *(Event, Icon)*
- Trained by **the Black Knives, the halfling assassins' guild** of **Glitterhaegen** *(Organization, Place)*

These backgrounds also tie nicely into icon relationships and One Unique Things. Maybe the Diabolist wants to capture the escaped PC and imprison them on the cursed pirate ship for good. Perhaps the character is the only person who clearly remembers what happened during the Emperor's 35th birthday party. Maybe they are the only human ever trained by the halfling assassin's guild. Every background is an opportunity for the player to present a story they would like to see unfold during the game.

DEALING WITH THE +5 "I'M GOOD AT EVERYTHING" BACKGROUND

What stops a player from putting the maximum number of points into a background called "I'm Good at Everything," allowing their PC to use a +5 bonus any time they roll a skill check?

Okay, maybe it's not quite as blatant as that. Maybe the player gave her character a +5 background called, "Elite Assassin of the Morning Star Guild" and insists on applying that bonus to every action, explaining that the Morning Star Guild trains its members to handle all possible situations.

Here's what distinguishes *13th Age* backgrounds from a list of specific skills: they're designed to create situations at the table in which the players have to exercise their creativity to solve a problem. Players tell the GM why their background applies to a skill check, if it's not obvious.

From this perspective, both the PC with the +5 background "Billionaire philanthropist crime fighter" and the PC with the +5 background "Five-time winner of the Archmage's annual snorkeling contest" have the same chance of applying that bonus to any given skill check. It depends on whether those players can make an entertaining and persuasive case for it. Having a "good at everything" background means the player will have to do that a lot.

We believe backgrounds are a matter of perspective, and some GMs may need to adjust the way they think about them. The fun they bring to the game is less about the actual bonus that helps a player's PC overcome some obstacle with a skill check, and much more about the stories that player tells over the course of campaign to justify why they are getting the bonus. Every story about "back in the monastery," for example, is providing worldbuilding details a GM can use to craft future stories, and information that gives everyone in the group a stronger sense of who that PC is, and that's a win-win.

That being said, there are ways to mitigate obvious ploys by players to get the bonus for nothing. First, always have the player narrate details about the background when it's being used for a skill check where failure comes with a high cost. For example, when failing to talk their way past the guards will result in capture and imprisonment. Or failing to bring down the wards means explosive runes will fry the heroes. Many groups get into the habit of handwaving background stories when it's obvious that the background would apply (or even just handwaving them in general), but the players have to earn it when something is truly on the line.

Another option is that you don't always have to give a player the full value of their background bonus. Perhaps they narrate a story about how being the Emperor's birthday organizer helps them to scale a sheer cliff thanks to stories the imperial climber told them at the party. Okay, they made an effort, but really? Hearing stories? Don't give them the +5 bonus, that background story is worth +1 or maybe +2 at best if they told the tale well. Or even just say no, it's too much of a stretch.

Yes, this does mean those players with a gift for spinning tales might have some advantage in skill check situations thanks to their +5 general background, but is the game truly worse for it? Most likely those stories are entertaining everyone. If not, and the rest of the players are getting annoyed by it, another way to rein that background in is to have the player break it into multiple, more specific backgrounds. This creates more limitations on what's possible, and means the bonus for each one is smaller and thus has less impact.

One GM summarized use of backgrounds perfectly in our eyes:

Is my background too powerful or useful? Only if it annoys the other players.

Is my background too weak or useless? Only if it annoys the other players.

I rarely have a player try to create a good-at-everything background. Maybe that's because when someone does create one, I hassle them every game session with NPCs who are related to their history, magic items that don't function exactly right because the PC is already so-good-at-everything, and other storytelling signs that they have painted a target on themselves. In other words, Cal and Wade have given you the Good GM *advice for handling this, and I'm here to represent the* Nasty GM.

CREATING MEMORABLE NPCS

Player characters live, fight, plunder, and carouse in a world populated with NPCs. Some of them are foes, with combat abilities designed to make them worthy of an adventurers' steel. But most of the people they encounter play smaller roles: the corrupt gatekeeper, the flinty merchant, the world-weary tavern keeper, and many others. NPCs appear in a session because they move the adventure forward by providing the PCs with resources or challenges. Sometimes they perform both functions: if the PCs encounter a gatekeeper who must be bribed or intimidated to let the party into the city, they've learned something important about the city and how it operates.

In this section, we'll offer advice on creating and statting NPCs. We've also provided ready-to-use NPCs, grouped by their suggested icon affiliation and designed to fit easily into a *13th Age* game set in the Dragon Empire—or with some tinkering, any fantasy setting. These characters fulfill small but necessary roles, ranging from buying and selling goods to digging graves and keeping the keys to the castle safe (or failing to do so).

Each NPC entry includes a brief description; a monster role and initiative to help you build them out using the *13th Age* DIY monster rules; and Three Things about the character's mannerisms, habits, or speech. Some of these characters know each other, and may even have family ties or romances.

NPC STATS

NPC stats depend on what level the NPC is, and whether they are an ally or an enemy. An NPC's level and abilities may change over the course of the campaign, especially as the NPC plays different roles relative to the party.

Stats for allies: If the NPC joins the party and fights alongside them, base their attack bonuses, defenses, and hit points on a typical member of that class. The NPC probably is about the same level as the members of the adventuring group. It's tricky to add a higher-level NPC to a group without having them outshine the PCs. Give the NPC a restricted list of powers and talents rather than the full complement that a PC would get. When an NPC joins the party for a battle, even if it's only one fight, define the NPC's abilities narrowly enough to make sure they don't crowd any of the PCs. If the NPC sticks to basic or at-will attacks, they will still add a lot of firepower and hit points to the group, so they'll be valuable even if they're not on par with the rest of the party. Special powers that provide bonuses and benefits to the PCs are also good choices.

Stats for enemies: Set the NPC's level at the PCs' level or a little higher, and use stats for a double-strength monster rather than a PC. By default, give the NPC an attack ability or two that allows them to target two enemies or make two attacks at half the normal strike damage amount, which plays better than a single attack for full strike damage. Adjust initiative, defenses, and hit points as you see fit to match the way you portray the NPC. Each NPC also has a number of abilities that are designed to work regardless of the NPC's level, and you should feel free add your own, as well.

Racial abilities: NPCs don't necessarily have racial abilities. Feel free to give a major NPC the same once-per-battle racial ability that the PCs enjoy (or even something better) if it makes them more impressive, or a more challenging opponent, but don't feel obligated to do so. In your version of the Dragon Empire, maybe not every high elf in the world can teleport—only the extraordinary ones.

BRINGING NPCS TO LIFE

NPCs can easily be made richer and more memorable by giving them a few distinctive qualities—what we call Three Things—that provide them with vivid personality traits; a distinctive appearance, voice, or even smell; and specific behaviors. For example, think of a certain huge, musclebound comic book character: he's green with torn purple pants, he smashes things, and he talks in monosyllables. You know exactly who we're talking about, and chances are, that's how you'd describe him from memory to someone who'd never heard of him.

Memorable NPCs can become recurring characters, and even rise to become major characters depending on how the story develops. The corrupt gatekeeper might be the resident spy for the Orc Lord, skulking around the PCs to discover how much of a threat they'll be to his plans; or he might turn out to be the one surprisingly steadfast ally the PCs have in a city riddled with evil. Heck, he might even be the Prince of Shadows. (Note: *Anyone* could be the Prince of Shadows.)

A fun way to make this happen is to follow the players' instincts regarding a character. If they automatically mistrust a priest of the Light who offers to heal them, hey—maybe that priest is actually the villain in the adventure. This gives the players the satisfaction of saying later, "I knew we couldn't trust that guy!"

ARCHMAGE

NPCs associated with the Archmage perform the same functions that others do, but they operate in a very different world: a stable hand can saddle a griffin without losing an arm, and a tailor knows which seemingly innocent designs one must *never* embroider into the hem of a wizard's robe.

The Chakta Ren

A supplier of magical necessities.

Normal caster [HUMANOID]
Initiative: +6

Sometimes, casters require things that you can't find in ordinary shops. *Special* things. Whether it's a single flake of skin from a Koru behemoth, a drop of sweat from a boar demon's brow, or ashes from the burned-down palace of the Wizard King, the Chakta Ren has what you need—or can tell you where to get it. You can purchase many of these things with coin—but rarer items come at a steeper price. Perhaps it's a small quest, or a large one. Perhaps it's all of your recoveries for the rest of the day. Or maybe you're willing to simply owe the Chakta Ren a favor. . . .

Three Things about the Chakta Ren

1: Dragonic with shimmering green and purple scales, and eyes that change color depending on its mood.
2: Handles all the items in its shop with obvious reverence and care, regardless of value.
3: Likes to point out the origins and craft of the PCs' true magic items. ("Ah! That bracelet is clearly from the 6th Age, and judging by the curve of the peacock's beak in the engraving, is the work of Borgflumindel of Achen—or one of her students.")

Frogknob

Normal caster [HUMANOID]
Initiative: +4

Most janitors don't have to know how to clean up spilled golem powder, get muttering oil stains out of the rug, and scrub the Cauldron of Seven Thousand Mysteries—all without being turned into the next "created by a mad wizard" species of monster. But Frogknob does, and much more besides. He's learned how to go about his business so as not to disturb a wizard's concentration, and as a result he's heard many secrets.

Three Things about Frogknob

1: Half-elf of indeterminate age with a pointed reddish beard and calloused hands, wearing a magically spotless blue tunic.
2: Physical features randomly change due to exposure to magical waste products: eyes change color, nose disappears, ears turn into bat wings or tiny silver trumpets that play music, and so on.
3: Occasionally a quiet *ribbit* can be heard coming from the vicinity of his trousers.

CRUSADER

Few NPCs connected with the Crusader are sitting on the fence when it comes to their patron's goals and methods. Among them you'll find steely-eyed fanatics, terrified minions looking to escape, and characters who are deeply conflicted about the morality of their actions.

Quartermaster Viga

Normal troop [HUMANOID]
Initiative: +4

An army marches on its stomach, even one that's backed by the power of dark gods. Viga is one of those officers responsible for keeping the Crusader's battalions supplied with food and equipment, and she has no time or patience for those who get in the way. As far as Viga is concerned, the Crusader's war is everyone's war, and every Imperial citizen should be eager to offer up food, lodging, horses, or anything else the Crusader needs to defeat the Diabolist. If not, maybe they want the Diabolist to win. . . .

Three Things about Viga

1: Half-orc with long, glossy black hair braided with bits of metal and bone.
2: Three fingers on her right hand were bitten off by a demon in battle.
3: Doesn't drink, but constantly chews a leaf that she claims acts as a stimulant.

Inquisitor Noj

Normal spoiler [HUMANOID]
Initiative: +6

Not all of the Crusader's foes look like monsters and meet his forces openly on the field of battle. Some of them are innocent-looking shopkeepers, farmers, and even high-ranking government officials. When the Crusader's armies arrive, Inquisitor Noj is with them, asking questions and going through local records to seek out and destroy the corruption within the community. Fortunately, good citizens of the Empire often come forward and bravely tell Noj about the suspicious activities of their neighbors and business rivals.

Three Things about Noj

1: Short, emaciated elf in a threadbare scholar's robe, white hair closely cropped like a soldier's.

2: If his skin becomes exposed, you see healed brands, scars from blades and whips, and wounds that a PC familiar with torture recognizes as marks left from being suspended by hooks.
3: Passionate about tea, and complains about the difficulty of finding proper brew when traveling.

Diabolist

The Diabolist draws an odd array of followers, some who are evil, some who are broken, and some who are dangerously eccentric. Given that the paths they're on always ends with more demons being let into the world, wise adventurers will treat all of them as if they were unexploded bombs.

Brother Simeon (Magus Astra)

Normal caster [HUMANOID]
Initiative: +4

There are those in the Empire who seek light in darkness, wisdom in madness, and holiness in depravity. Such a one is Brother Simeon, a priest of Light whose bland appearance and solid respectability conceals a brilliant mind aflame with the pursuit of forbidden knowledge and extreme experiences. As "Magus Astra," he is famous throughout the Diabolist's hidden networks of magical practitioners as an innovator who pushes the bounds of reality through his writing, art, and blasphemous rituals.

Three Things about Simeon

1: Gnome with large, pale, watery eyes and wisps of dark hair clinging damply to his perspiring scalp.
2: Has high, fluting, monotonous voice that threatens to send all of his listeners to sleep (but which comes alive with intensity and gleeful menace when he is free to reveal himself as Magus Astra).
3: Always has a drowsy, disinterested white opossum with him that he calls Childers (actually a highly intelligent demonic familiar).

Kuljani Proost

Normal troop [HUMANOID]
Initiative: +8

Kuljani's parents served the Diabolist fanatically until they were torn apart by summoned demons. Kuljani's mother was pregnant with her at the time, and the Diabolist claims to have personally delivered Kuljani alive from her dead mother's womb. Raised in a hellhole by cultists and demons, Kuljani became a violent, emotionally unstable assassin—but deep down in her twisted soul, she longs to escape her life and find a loving family. Maybe she's still an assassin in your campaign, working undercover in a tavern, stable, or scullery frequented by her latest target; or maybe she fled her handlers, and is on the run from the Diabolist's agents.

Three Things about Kuljani

1: Human with long, tangled, ash-blonde hair and eyes bright with madness.
2: In moments of stress, mutters abyssal chants to comfort herself.
3: Is a masterful baker, an art that she learned as a child from a demon of gluttony.

Dwarf King

Many fantasy stories and settings present dwarves as a race for whom honor and family bonds are vitally important. The lives of these NPCs are intertwined in ways that might be confusing to non-dwarves, and deeply complicated by matters of pride and obligation.

Maxim Goldfinder, Slava's Son, Yelena's Husband

Normal leader [HUMANOID]
Initiative: +5

Maxim and his wife Yelena own the nearby gold mine, and are pillars of both the local dwarven and Imperial communities. Unusually, they live in the wealthy district of town side by side with humans, instead of in the tight-knit dwarven enclave. He trusts his enslaved bond-servant Borys with all things (including his life), and clearly has the utmost respect and affection for Yelena.

Three Things about Maxim

1: A richly dressed dwarf, powerfully built with a thick, blonde beard and rings flashing from his fingers.
2: Courteous but cunning, often answering questions with, "It is a dwarf thing, outsiders cannot understand," and refusing to commit to an agreement or course of action until he is confident that it is not a trap.
3: His magic hammer Dealmaker (which adds a bonus to the wielder's negotiating and diplomacy checks) is always either on his person, or on display within reach.

Yelena Spearfighter, Rufina's Daughter, Maxim's Wife

Normal leader [HUMANOID]
Initiative: +6

Yelena likes to tell the story of how she proposed to Maxim after splitting the skull of a bugbear that was about to cleave him in two. Maxim argues that it was a hobgoblin, not a bugbear, but it's obvious that the dwarf spear-fighter is a force to be reckoned with. Yelena is universally admired for her good humor, generosity, and courage, and has earned the respect of even her deadliest enemies. Life is quieter now that she and Maxim have settled in town and are busy running the mine, and sometimes she yearns for the wild freedom of battle.

Three Things about Yelena

1: A richly dressed dwarf, powerfully built with long, glossy black hair, a mischievous smile, and a gold medallion bearing a rune that roughly means, "Touch my stuff and you'll lose an arm."
2: Eagerly offers hospitality and help to anyone in need.
3: Invites guests to spar with her in the courtyard of their mansion, though she rarely meets her match.

Nikolai Treefeller, Ivan's Son, Yelena's Brother

Normal spoiler [HUMANOID]
Initiative: +4

A dwarf who runs a lumber camp, instead of delving in the earth or shaping rock and metal? Depending on your campaign, Nikolai's occupation might be a mark of failure that infects his soul with bitterness and envy, leaving him vulnerable to the honeyed promises of the Diabolist; or he might be one of the rare dwarves who feels more kinship with the High Druid than the Dwarf King.

Three Things about Nikolai

1: A modestly dressed dwarf, slightly built with long, glossy black hair and beard tied into braids
2: Prone to long digressions about different types of trees and their suitability for different types of projects.
3: Becomes agitated and defensive when stereotypical dwarven pursuits (mining, smithing, etc.) come up in conversation.

Elf Queen

NPCs connected to the Elf Queen live half in this world, half in the world of the fey. Whether this is literally another realm, or just another way of being, the lives of the Elf Queen's people are filled with the stuff of legends, fairy tales, and myths: swords rise out of the lakes they pass, and riddling trolls live under the bridges they cross. Their obligations must be fulfilled no matter what it takes, and their loves are either grand and heartbreaking, or as fleeting as moonlight.

Aiken Crow

Normal spoiler [HUMANOID]
Initiative: +6

The stories and rumors contradict each other: Is Aiken Crow a man, a woman, or something else? Foolish, or wise? Lazy, or driven? Trustworthy, or the most treacherous creature who ever walked the Empire? Maybe everything is true, or none of it. This wandering fey appears in unlikely places with strange tidings, good advice, and bad jokes in equal measure.

Three Things about Aiken

1: A tall elf, all knees and elbows, dressed in colorful patchwork clothes, with unkempt red hair and alert brown eyes.
2: Refers to self in the third person and often speaks in rhyme.
3: A ravenous eater who offers valuable information in exchange for food, but those who refuse to feed Aiken find that their supplies get lost, spoiled, or stolen later.

Skara of the Green Hills

Large troop [HUMANOID]
Initiative: +4

If something big needs to be lifted, carried, or smashed, the Elf Queen's folk know to whistle for Skara. In all her years—she forgets her age, but assumes that it's a lot of years—she's only met one object that she couldn't overcome by strength and dogged determination (and it's probably something the PCs are either looking for, or trying to remove).

Three Things about Skara

1: An ogre dressed in orc skins, carrying a massive club that she calls "Charlie."
2: At any mention of orcs, she eagerly asks if the PCs could arrange a wrestling match between her and the Orc Lord, whom she's sure she could beat if given the chance.
3: Has a birthmark on her right buttock which marks her as a legitimate heir to the Imperial throne (according to her).

Emperor

The Emperor represents structure, authority, order, and just rule. Although NPCs connected with the Emperor can occupy any role, this seems like a good place to introduce some representatives of the ruling class whom the PCs are likely to encounter.

Count Garrett

Normal leader [HUMANOID]
Initiative: +7

A decorated war hero, Garrett was granted military authority over an important border province—depending on your campaign, he might stand between the citizens of the Empire and the forces of the Three, the Orc Lord, the Diabolist, or even the High Druid. Garrett is a brave man and a devoted husband to the countess, courteous and generous toward both ally and enemy. But he is also a flawed man, and soon to be tested.

Three Things about Garrett

1: A stocky human with close-cropped dark hair going to gray, in a red tunic and gold cloak.
2: Wears an eyepatch embroidered with the symbol of the Emperor in gold thread, a gift from the icon in recognition of the count's deeds in the conflict that cost him that eye.
3: An avid knowledge seeker who will gladly discuss books and lore, and grants suitably learned PCs access to his impressive library.

Countess Landina

Normal leader [HUMANOID]
Initiative: +8

A military strategist in the Elf Queen's army, Landina was assigned by the icon to work with an Imperial general who arrived one day at the Court of Stars to humbly ask for the elves' help in an upcoming battle. Her counsel led to several decisive victories, and the two quickly formed a close bond that went far beyond their professional relationship. It was Landina who dragged Garrett's unconscious body from the battle where he lost his eye, and the pair have been inseparable since then. Lately, though, she has begun to develop strong feelings for another member of their household.

Three Things about the Countess

1: A lean, athletic half-elf with hair in an intricate weave often found among certain wood elf tribes, dressed in sober, dark clothes and wearing a silver ring given by the Elf Queen.
2: Pauses before speaking as she weighs her words carefully.
3: When not dealing with matters of office, likes to retreat to someplace private and play sad songs of the elves on a silvery flute.

Other Members of the Count and Countess's Household

Their children, Nord, Helga and Tiritia
Ansdell the gamekeeper
Wringa the steward (in charge of running the household overall)
Forningas the chamberlain (in charge of seeing to the needs of the count and countess and their family)
Frotberga the chief cook
Ingalbertus the butler (in charge of beer, wine and ale)
Lambertus the pantler (in charge of the pantry)
Rhaina the marshal (in charge of stables, horses, carts, wagons, and containers)
Heldall watch-captain of the castle guards

Great Gold Wyrm

NPCs connected to the Great Gold Wyrm are found in surprising places. But regardless of who they are and what they do, they exhibit the qualities of duty, humility, and self-sacrifice on behalf of the greater good.

Kyffin Lews

Normal troop [HUMANOID]
Initiative: +5

It's hard to be a proper street thief and pickpocket when you keep hearing your dear mum's voice in your ears, reciting the teachings of the Great Gold Wyrm. Kyffin is a skilled rogue who does what he needs to survive and prosper in the slums where he lives, and he dreams of someday being a powerful crime lord—but he tries to only rob those who do wrong, and finds himself reluctantly using most of his ill-gotten gains to help others in need.

Three Things about Kyffin

1: Human of medium height and dark features, with large, bright eyes and curly brown hair, dressed to blend in wherever he happens to be.
2: Boasts of his future prospects and all the fine things he someday plans to buy with his loot, once he makes a big enough score.
3: When worried or deep in thought, rubs a medallion of the Great Gold Wyrm (given to him by his late mother) with his thumb—and woe to anyone who steals that item from him.

Mingxia, Scourge of Demons (Deceased)

Normal leader [UNDEAD]
Initiative: +8

Mingxia's deeds in her final battle ring across the ages: how she and her magic sword Cleansing Sun cut down a hundred demons with every stroke, and broke the power of that age's Diabolist at the cost of her own life. But her spirit remains—perhaps bound to her tomb, or wandering the field of that last battle, or haunting the halls of her castle. If a PC with a positive relationship with the Great Gold Wyrm asks for her help in the name of the icon, she will honor her ancient vow and do whatever she can.

Three Things about Mingxia

1: Human ghost, compact and muscular, dressed in ornate, battle-dented armor, with her long black hair tied in a bun.
2: Speaks to PCs with the ease and informality of a fellow adventurer, and might suggest going out for a drink at the tavern and swapping tales before remembering that she's a ghost.
3: Can provide useful knowledge about things that existed during her Age, such as an ancient monster's weakness, how to bypass a difficult obstacle in a dungeon, or the secret history of another NPC's family line.

High Druid

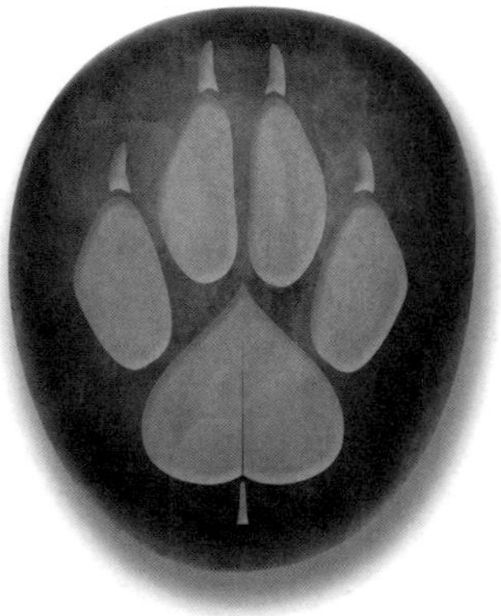

Are the High Druid's followers enlightened beings living in harmony with nature? Or creepy fanatics who can't wait to show you the inside of the wicker man they've built in the sacred grove?

Nigesa of the River

Normal caster [HUMANOID]
Initiative: +4

Nigesa has seen what happens when civilization tramples and poisons the wilderness, and she is determined to prevent it from happening again. She speaks for the Wild with passionate words in the courts of the powerful, and with equally powerful actions: sabotaging destructive mining and logging operations, smelters and refineries, and more. She bears a special grudge against wizards for their experiments on animals.

Three Things about Nigesa

1: Dark-skinned half elf in blue traveling clothes, with blue glass beads in her braided hair.
2: Wears necklaces, bracelets and anklets of wood and horn which sound like river water rushing over rocks when she walks.
3: Speaks calmly and deliberately, only betraying anger and impatience with a raised eyebrow—addresses people as "Child of . . ." (For example, a dwarf might be "Child of stone," an elf might be "Child of stars," a ranger might be "Child of the deep woods," and so on.)

Lord Osa

Normal leader [HUMANOID]
Initiative: +4

Lord Osa gladly welcomes adventurers to his happy realm. In the old days, he and his people starved because they followed the false teachings of the Priestess, Emperor, and Archmage. But in the decades since Lord Osa led his people in a return to the old ways—the ways of their ancestors in the ages before ages were numbered—the spirits of the earth have blessed their lands with prosperity.

Three Things about Lord Osa

1: Dark-skinned human in red robes, with gold rings on his fingers and a medallion with an ancient druidic symbol on it.
2: Has a rich, deep singing voice and enjoys entertaining guests with songs he's learned from the spirits.
3: Will offer the PCs anything they need that is within his power—but forbids them from doing one thing while they are guests in his realm. (It's up to you what that thing is, and whether Lord Osa is a villain hiding a terrible secret or a

hero trying to keep the PCs from unleashing something nasty.)

Lich King

Here's an interesting thing about the Lich King and NPCs: wherever the PCs go in your campaign, they will find dead (or soon to be dead) people. And wherever there are dead people, there are those whose job is to ensure that the dead don't rise from the grave and join the Lich King's ranks. Among the hazards of working with the dead for so long is that one tends to develop certain sympathies with them, and their undying lord. . . .

Peacock

Normal troop [HUMANOID]
Initiative: +1

Peacock is a gravedigger; which is to say, gravedigger is her profession, but it is also her family name, which one might think strange, since none of them were of the grave-digging profession; and if the PCs have but a moment, she will relate the delightful tale of how that came to be, starting with a distant ancestor name of "Dayve Grigger." If the PCs can get her to stop telling pointless stories, she can tell them who is buried where, and she knows the histories of those whom she's buried. She is fond of macabre riddles and word games, and periodically thumps her assistant Livesey alongside the head for his clumsy work.

Three Things about Peacock

1: Halfling with turned-up nose and large ears, both of which she frequently digs in with her pinky.
2: Likes to sing raucous tavern songs as she works, and, if her singing is remarked upon, will insist on showing you the accompanying knees-up dance.
3: Has a mole on her belly that's shaped like an owl, or maybe it's a camel or octopus.

Skeli Mord

Normal spoiler [HUMANOID]
Initiative: +1

Skeli Mord is a most humble and sympathetic purveyor of funeral supplies, including coffins, urns, and headstones. He is grateful for the opportunity to help you send your hated enemy into the next world with all the contempt that they deserve. Oh—they were a loved one? Are you sure that you didn't hate them, even a little bit? Well, whatever your needs, Skeli Mord is here to assist at very reasonable prices.

Three Things

1: Long-nosed dark elf with shoulder-length silver hair wearing robes and a shapeless velvet hat of deep crimson.
2: Wears a silver betrothal chain, even though he slew his beloved a hundred years ago during a war between their rival families (an elf or other PC with knowledge of the Silver Folk will recognize the chain's significance).
3: When irritated, unconsciously taps a dark elf marching rhythm with his fingers.

Ailwyn Grieve

Normal troop [HUMANOID]
Initiative: +4

Ailwyn Grieve is an Imperial thanatologist. Death is her field of study—and with the Lich King constantly seeking new minions, it is a matter of Imperial security. She is an expert in the funerary customs of all races and regions, including the rituals and materials needed to prevent the dead from rising, and the construction and safeguarding of graves, tombs, and mausoleums. She views necromancers with extreme suspicion.

Three Things about Ailwyn

1: A surprisingly cheerful human, given her occupation—solidly built with curly brown hair and ruddy cheeks.
2: Gives everyone nicknames because she can never remember the names of living people, only the dead.

3: You can hear her coming because she's whistling a children's nursery song that sounds awfully creepy somehow.

Orc Lord

The chief questions for NPCs connected with the Orc Lord are, when will he launch his assault on the Empire, what will he destroy, and what are his odds of winning? Depending on their conclusions, they're either helping ensure the Orc Lord's victory, or figuring out how to escape with their own skins intact (and maybe even profit).

Thurash Many Rocks, Smasher of Elves

Normal troop [HUMANOID]
Initiative: +6

Many half orcs are loyal citizens of the Empire, ready to fight the

Orc Lord's forces in defense of civilization. Thurash is not one of them. To him the Orc Lord is the agent of revolution—a force of historical inevitability who will burn the weak, corrupt Empire with cleansing fire, and establish a new age, and a new empire. Until that day, Thurash will do his part by serving as a spy within the Imperial system, presenting a loyal façade while gathering intelligence and recruiting sympathizers.

Three Things about Thurash

1: Tall, powerfully muscled half-orc with long, lustrous hair and seven gold earrings (three in the left ear, four on the right).

2: Collects orcish items such as weapons, gear, and artwork as a way of staying connected with his orcish heritage.

3: Smells pleasantly of sandalwood.

Althea Wainwright

Normal leader [HUMANOID]
Initiative: +2

Althea, head of one of the Dragon Empire's most powerful shipping and transport companies, has received reports from the northwest frontier and sees the writing on the wall: the Orc Lord is coming, and nobody is ready for him. Her concerns fell on deaf ears—what would a mere merchant know of military matters?—so she's decided to take advantage of the situation as best she can. She's negotiated safe passage through areas controlled by the Orc Lord in exchange for allowing certain caravans to be "robbed," thus supplying those orc tribes with high quality weapons, armor, and other goods. When war comes, maybe she'll use what she knows to help the Empire. Or maybe she'll just disappear and retire to a nice village somewhere far away.

Three Things about Althea

1: Stiff-backed human with a hawk-like nose, gray hair pulled back in a bun, wearing rich clothes in purple, gray, and black with the sign of her house subtly embroidered on them.

2: Friendly toward rangers, dwarves, and others who seem to know something about either travel (land, sea, and air) or crafting quality goods.

3: Knows something about pretty much anywhere the PCs have ever been, and will gladly offer information as long as it doesn't threaten her operation.

Priestess

Not all those who serve the Priestess appear wreathed in glory, wielding hammers and healing spells. Some are cloaked in humility—but play a vital role in keeping the Light burning in a dark world.

The Lady of the Steps

Normal caster [HUMANOID]
Initiative: +2

Few hurrying to and from the merchant houses and halls of government notice the Lady who sits on the steps in the public square, feeding the birds and begging for alms. But she notices them, and sees their destinies written on them as plain as ink. She is the oracle of the tradesfolk and the poor, who seek her insights in exchange for hot meals, warm blankets, bread for her birds, and their assistance in helping someone else in trouble.

Three Things about the Lady

1: A woman of indeterminate age and race, dressed in layers of cast-off clothes that she washes in a nearby fountain, and a wide-brimmed floppy hat that shields her from the elements.

2: When she speaks, her voice is high and raspy, with a sing-song storyteller's cadence.

3: Occasionally coughs into a rag, leaving spots of bright, glowing fluid.

Nutripher Fantastikon, King of Wrongway

Normal troop [HUMANOID]
Initiative: +1

Some who have seen his paintings describe them as a window into a spiritual realm of a transcendent hope and beauty—but many more say they're pointless blobs and scrawls of color that any child could create. Everyone agrees that the artist who calls himself Nutripher Fantastikon is eccentric, perhaps even mad. But discerning PCs with a positive or conflicted relationship with the Priestess will see that the painter's admirers are more right than they know: Fantastikon's canvases are literal windows into the realm of the gods of Light, and through them, a connection to the Cathedral.

Three Things about Nutripher

1: A gnome with a huge moustache, elaborately waxed and curled, dressed in what at first glance appears to be the clothes of a rich merchant or noble, but are actually cheap theater costumes.

2: "Rides" a toy stick-horse he calls Dauntless (which may or may not transform into a divine war-steed if necessary).

3: Prone to issuing royal proclamations and bestowing knighthoods.

PRINCE OF SHADOWS

The Prince of Shadows? Never heard of him, officer.

LADY NIGHTWHISPER

Normal caster [HUMANOID]
Initiative: +7

The heroic deeds of the PCs made them noteworthy for a while, but these days the public's attention is captured by the mysterious masked swordswoman known as Lady Chasmodia Nightwhisper. The news sheets breathlessly relate her latest daring exploits. Children playing in the streets pretend to be her, acting out swordfights with sticks. Decorated black masks have become fashionable among the wealthy and powerful. Yes, Lady Nightwhisper is more dashing, skilled, cunning and . . . well, just better than the PCs. Maybe she's just as she seems: a competent rival who will give the party a run for their money, but might be an ally when their interests converge. Or maybe one day, after she's gained the trust of her targets, "Lady Nightwhisper" will disappear forever, leaving behind an empty treasury vault. . . .

THREE THINGS ABOUT LADY NIGHTWHISPER

1: Appears to be a young halfling woman with black hair and bright green eyes, dressed in a black military hat, tunic, and trousers tucked into high, soft black boots, with a swirling black cloak, and a eye-mask made of black silk decorated with black-on-black images of dragons.
2: Has a flamboyant, cocky manner, as though she's always just on the verge of revealing a stunning surprise.
3: Prone to wagering, and is a gracious loser—or appears to be.

OLEG "THE OWLBEAR" STONEGRINDER

Normal leader [HUMANOID]
Initiative: +5

Did Oleg Stonecrusher, alleged crime boss, really tear off an underling's arm just for spilling a single drop of blood on his boots? Yes, he did. Does Oleg have a hidden sentimental, kind side that balances out his savagery? Not that anyone is aware of. Unlike some crime figures who prefer to stay in one heavily guarded location, Oleg is always on the go—keeping his "fortress" (as he calls it) around him in the form of visible bodyguards and disguised assassins armed with hidden blowguns. Oleg does enjoy a good story, particularly if it involves someone foolish dying violently.

THREE THINGS ABOUT OLEG

1: Broad-shouldered, large-bellied dwarf wearing a leather jerkin and purple cloak, with his moustache and the tip of his beard dyed bright red.
2: Wears a new pair of gleaming, expensive black leather boots every day.
3: Breath smells powerfully of onions, which he eats with every meal in the belief that it wards off evil spirits.

THE THREE

Watch out for NPCs connected with the Three: they rarely work alone. If you kill a sorcerer, get ready to be hunted by a sinister monk assassin and a red-scaled dragonic barbarian.

AGRABATH FLAMESKULL

Normal troop [HUMANOID]
Initiative: +3

Flameskull was a tough son of a gun back in the old days, cleaving and decapitating dozens of foes while roaring the war-cry of the Red. But inevitably, age and battle took its toll. Flameskull retired to the outskirts of a small village, where he lives quietly and mainly keeps to himself. He acts the part of a gruff soldier; but he lives in secret terror of the possibility that the Red will call him into service again.

THREE THINGS ABOUT AGRABATH

1: Heavily scarred, red-scaled dragonic dressed in simple farmer's clothes, with a large dent in his head from a dwarven hammer.
2: If the PCs overcome his initial suspicion, he is eager to talk about adventuring and war with someone who's been there, unlike the farmers and merchants he lives among.
3: Suffers from trauma that manifests as nightmares and terrified paralysis when in danger.

RABENNA QUEAL

Normal caster [HUMANOID]
Initiative: +4

As a sorcerer, Rabenna Queal is not especially powerful. But as a mercenary she has the advantage of complete amorality: no job is too low, dirty, or despicable if your gold is good. Queal has an uncanny knack for survival, returning intact from massacres demanding the rest of her pay. If you need to know who's hiring adventurers, and which ones to avoid, you could do worse than to consult her. On the other hand, she tends to forget that others have standards—and jobs that she recommends might lead to disaster.

Three Things about Rabenna

1: Ash-pale, thin and sickly human, with leather armor, black and grey traveling clothes, and dragonic eyes from prolonged exposure to sorcery.
2: Lets out a high-pitched giggle when nervous.
3: Worries that she needs a better wand.

Ahn Kyung-Jae

Normal spoiler [HUMANOID]
Initiative: +8

Ahn Curiosities is a small shop that would be easy to miss, were it not for the flag hanging out front with the coiling black dragon on it. PCs will find an assortment of rare items, at least one of which will happen to be something minor but immediately useful—a scroll case to protect a recently acquired map, polish for newly upgraded armor, or high-quality outdoor cookware that's perfect for a character with a background as a chef. Ahn Kyung-Jae is amiable and blandly polite. He is also the front man for a local league of assassins in service to the Black—a PC with a positive relationship with the Three will spot the signs, and can use icon roll results to gain his assistance.

Three Things about Ahn

1: Stout human of medium build, balding with stubby fingers, dressed in a black, red, and blue robe.
2: Whistles a tune while he sweeps the front stoop of his shop—the tune, and the pattern of his sweeping, send a coded message to the Black's local network of followers.
3: Likes to talk business over a plate of pastries from the shop next door.

Six Things Rob Does Now

We like making lists of thirteen. But sometimes I don't have thirteen things worth saying.

Here are six things I do when I'm running *13th Age* that I didn't do until I'd been running the game awhile. A couple of them may be things you've been doing forever. A couple others will be new to most of you.

Big trouble: Sometimes I set up an overwhelming battle and start the initiative die at 1. Basically the PCs realize they could be in serious trouble, and adrenaline kicks them up a notch from the start.

Since most of the battles I run for my home tables are quite difficult compared to the building battles table, it has to be something pretty extreme to qualify for starting with the escalation die.

Daily icons: Sometimes I only roll for icon relationship results once an adventuring day instead of at the start of each session. Cal and Wade have covered this option in detail elsewhere in the book.

Grab is a bit simpler, or at least different: I don't use the grab rules that are printed on pages 172 and 173 of the core rulebook any more. Here's the full rules for how I play grabs for monsters now.

The important bit is that when a monster that is grabbing you starts its turn, it deals automatic damage to you as a free action. The automatic damage is equal to half the normal damage that it deals with the attack that damaged you. For example, a glabrezou's *pincer* attack deals 45 damage, so the automatic damage when it has someone grabbed is 23 damage.

This automatic damage is in addition to the monster's normal actions and attacks.

When you are grabbed you are engaged with the creature grabbing you and you can't move away unless you teleport, somehow pop free, or successfully disengage.

If you are smaller than the creature that is grabbing you, it can move and carry you along no problem. If you are the same size or larger, the creature grabbing you has to let go of you if it wants to move.

And that's really all the extra rules that are needed. Obviously you want to get away when a monster has grabbed you, and the usual way you manage that is trying to disengage. But you can also just fight back and hope to drop them. Using a ranged attack when grabbed isn't fun because you're probably going to take an opportunity attack from being engaged, but that's just using the normal rules.

The min/max coin: Jonathan is happy when players choose to do average damage with their characters' attacks instead of rolling dice. I'm fine with whatever the player wants, and I also enjoyed tweaking Jonathan's idea by saying that my character will go one step further: I flip a coin. Tails is minimum damage, heads is maximum damage. I got so far ahead on these coin flips that I gave it up and went back to rolling damage, declining to regress toward the mean! The fact that I'm proud of this is just a little sad.

When a player wants to do average damage, I give them the option of flipping the min/max coin. Do you feel lucky?

The opening cut: Sometimes I start action with a confrontation between one or two characters and one or two monsters/NPCs. It's not a surprise round, per se, because they're not blasting uninvolved creatures with spells, it's a quick exchange of blows between the acting creatures, as if the other characters weren't in the scene. These are the first cuts or blasts between suddenly active combatants, before anyone else gets involved. The two (or rarely, three or four) characters/creatures who acted in the confrontation round keep their initiative rolls, but once the actual combat begins they may have other PCs and monsters acting ahead of them.

As a rule, these opening cuts of battle doesn't count for raising the escalation die. The first real round of combat comes after everyone has rolled initiative.

Pre-fight meditation: It's a GM thing. I always try to think about what roleplaying moments might develop during a fight before I tell everyone to roll initiative, or immediately after the action has started while the players are sorting out the scene for themselves. It's not that I'm going to make sure any of the things happen, but it helps to start with a notion that there are moments and characters and interactions that could have storytelling and roleplay consequences for particular characters aside from the straight combat mechanics. Every once in a while, an unexpected development in the midst of combat ends up turning the fight from a dramatic conflict to something people are going to remember forever. Icon relationships might or might not be involved.

13 Bits of GM Advice from Other Books

Advice that seems worth repeating, even if you noticed it the first time around.

Combat Crunch

If you want more combat modifiers than *13th Age* uses, feel free to port bonuses in from another system and use those. Another option, however, is to invent special and unique sources for combat bonuses. It's more interesting to get a +2 bonus to your attacks because you're a dwarf fighting in the ancient dwarven Hall of Blood, or because you have probed your enemy's weaknesses in its dreams than because you're flanking it. Also, make free use of the dazed and weakened conditions. If an effect is worth worrying about, it could be worth a 4-point swing in attacks or defenses.

Cursed Items

The point of cursed items, and especially cursed weapons, is that they provide a bonus that is superior to normal items at their tier. Some players adore that type of thing and willingly use cursed items because they think the math goes in their favor. Other players think those people are crazy. So this is an area where what players think is sometimes more important than what their characters think. If you prefer, treat cursed items as objects that can only be gotten rid of via complicated quests instead of relying on the power-greed of particular players.

Disengaging

In some particularly dramatic circumstance, feel free to ignore the disengage rule in pursuit of a powerful story.

Evil PCs

You're under no obligation to allow truly evil player characters. Many tables can't handle the dysfunction. But some players can handle subtle or situational evil that allows them to function as a non-destructive part of a campaign.

Fleeing

Players just *love* to get stuck in dire circumstances from which, as a special exception, fleeing isn't an option. Be sure to tell the players when they are in a situation where there is no escape, because the game improves when you find ways of increasing the players' fear without necessarily increasing the threat. Half the point of giving the players a useful option like fleeing is so you can take it from them now and then.

Icons

Some GMs work out how all the icons are going to play out in their campaign. These GMs figure out the motivations of each icon, especially the ambiguous ones, and offer guidance when players are choosing icon relationships so that player choices work out well in the scope of the campaign.

Other GMs let the players take the first crack at the icons and build out their campaigns to suit what their players have in mind. These GMs are willing to work with a character's backstory that sounds far-fetched at first, adjusting the campaign background to incorporate elements of all the players' backstories.

We generally do a little pre-planning and offer guidance around the icon roles, followed by adjustment and retconning as the players create their *uniques* and backgrounds.

Killing Player Characters

Killing player characters is both a time-honored tradition and a huge headache for the GM. It can blow holes in the story when the guy who seemed to be the hero gets killed by Random Orc #53, but nothing captures the thrill and uncertainly of interactive fiction like having your character's survival depend on the dice and your wits.

Having been the softest, most forgiving gamemaster for years, Gareth Ryder-Hanrahan has come to believe that the benefits of PC death outweigh the problems. He still doesn't kill characters that often, and he'll let them survive if it makes for a more interesting story, but it's never wholly off the table.

Jonathan Tweet doesn't allow PCs to just die fighting nameless monsters. In fact, he likes the rule that PCs can only be fully slain by named villains. The bright side is that PCs who fail four death checks in his game don't die, they just fall into a coma and can't be brought back to consciousness during combat, only once they're fully out of danger. The dark side is that Jonathan's nameless NPCs are more than willing to take unconscious PCs to named villains for a proper ritual sacrifice.

One Unique Things

If players don't want to come up with a one unique thing right away, or if they want to give the game a chance to develop, it's fine to let some players feel their way into what is unique about their characters after the first or second session. This delay may come in especially handy if a player wants to figure out what the tone of the campaign is before settling on their big secret or special feature.

Rallying

Old-school GMs sometimes flinch at the idea that anyone can heal themselves without using magic. We don't swing that way because we like the idea that heroes can recover themselves—it suits heroic drama, and we think it makes a better game. We also think of hit points as having something to do with morale and will-to-fight instead of only bone and blood. But if your picture of your world doesn't include characters pulling themselves together in the middle of combat, ignore the rally rule, find other abilities for the races and classes that rely on it most, and make your PCs work for other methods of healing.

Recoveries

If you don't want to slow the game down while people figure out whether they are going to take average hit points with a recovery or roll it, ask each player for his or her recovery option beforehand and enforce that method until the party gets to a full heal-up.

Re-Rolls

We're not big on tormenting players by making them guess whether they hit before they decide whether to use abilities like rerolls. Keep the game moving by making hits and misses transparent. You can let players know the defense targets they're aiming for, if you wish, or keep the exact numbers secret but tell people right away whether they hit or missed.

Roll Multiple Saves?

Rolling multiple saves against ongoing effects that deal the same type of damage is easier on PCs because they're likely to save against at least part of the damage. Combining all the damage into one big save is more dramatic, and if you want to speed things up, feel free to combine saves.

Three Most Dangerous Dungeons

Consider having each campaign start with mention of that campaign's three most dangerous dungeons, living or otherwise. If you have played a d20 game before, and spent money on adventure material, you may already have a few pages or books of dungeons and dangerous locations. We contributed to such products in earlier work, and we draft whatever makes us happy for our games, so we advise shameless and eclectic dungeon-grafting.

ADVICE REMINDER INDEX

Here's a short list of other useful GM advice and where you can find it. For reference, 13C is the core book, 13TW is *13 True Ways*, B is the *13th Age Bestiary*, and EST is *Eyes of the Stone Thief*.

Iconic Allies, Enemies, and Follower Goals Cheatsheet

Use this sheet to track the PCs' icons, the icons they consider allies or enemies, and what the followers of those icons want from the PCs. (Permission to photocopy this page.)

Icon ____________________

Allied Icon 1: ____________________
What their followers want: ____________________

Allied Icon 2: ____________________
What their followers want: ____________________

Enemy Icon 1: ____________________
What their followers want: ____________________

Enemy Icon 2: ____________________
What their followers want: ____________________

Icon ____________________

Allied Icon 1: ____________________
What their followers want: ____________________

Allied Icon 2: ____________________
What their followers want: ____________________

Enemy Icon 1: ____________________
What their followers want: ____________________

Enemy Icon 2: ____________________
What their followers want: ____________________

Icon ____________________

Allied Icon 1: ____________________
What their followers want: ____________________

Allied Icon 2: ____________________
What their followers want: ____________________

Enemy Icon 1: ____________________
What their followers want: ____________________

Enemy Icon 2: ____________________
What their followers want: ____________________

Icon ____________________

Allied Icon 1: ____________________
What their followers want: ____________________

Allied Icon 2: ____________________
What their followers want: ____________________

Enemy Icon 1: ____________________
What their followers want: ____________________

Enemy Icon 2: ____________________
What their followers want: ____________________

The Archmage

has preserved the Empire for centuries and created astonishing new lands. He has also threatened the fabric of reality with experiments you'd have to be brilliant or hugely arrogant to attempt.

The Crusader

is the armored fist of the Dark Gods. So long as followers of the Gods of Light stay the hell out of his way, the Crusader turns his wrath against the demons that would destroy the world his own gods want to rule. Follow the Crusader if you must win at any cost.

The Diabolist

controls fiends and tampers with forces even the Archmage avoids. She likes her victims screaming and her chaos pure while claiming that the demons she summons would otherwise overwhelm the Great Gold Wyrm who seals the Abyss. There are two differences between her and her demons: First, she likes keeping destruction personal rather than universal. Second, she's capable of kindness, so long as it comes as a great surprise.

The Dwarf King

is lord of Forge, the dwarves' new homeland beneath the mountains. He'd love to reclaim the dwarven Underhome lost to war against the dark elves and the creatures of the deeps. But now that the Empire is stumbling, the dwarves find themselves manning the mountain walls that shield the Empire from the orcs and monsters of the north.

The Elf Queen

rules the Court of Stars, the one place where wood elves, dark elves, and high elves come together as peers and allies instead of as rivals or enemies. Honed by centuries of experience, the Queen's innate magic at least equals the Archmage's spells.

The Emperor

rules the world's greatest human kingdom, known as the Dragon Empire for the mounts of its mightiest warriors. All the signs suggest that the age is turning, but will the Empire fall or shift to a new balance?

The Great Gold Wyrm

is the world's protector and the inspiration for holy orders of paladins and independent heroes. Although the Gold Wyrm's physical form seals the gap that prevents the Abyss from erupting into the world, his dreams and the agents he employs still move through the world, helping those who will fight and even die for what's right.

The High Druid

is the champion of the resurgent Wild, and the spiritual and magical leader of spirits of nature and the elements that were chained by the Empire but are now working themselves free. She might be the great force that shakes the Empire to pieces or the hero who destroys the destroyers and points to a new way to live.

The Lich King

is the lord of the undead, a fallen tyrant who intends to conquer the Dragon Empire and restore his ancient kingdom. He's not entirely insane and mostly understands that ruling a kingdom is not the same as destroying it.

The Orc Lord

is a figure of legend. The last time he walked the land the Lich King fell, in part because of the Orc Lord's attack. Who will fall before his hordes this time? Who won't?

The Priestess

hears all the Gods of Light and speaks for those who please her. She is part oracle, part mystic, and part metaphysical engineer, since she created the Cathedral, an ever-expanding temple with rooms or entire wings for each of the faiths she favors.

The Prince of Shadows

is part thief, part trickster, and part assassin. To some he is a hero; to others a villain. He has squandered the riches of the dwarves, murdered the hopes of a dragon, and plundered the dreams of a god. His exploits have changed the world, but none can tell you his ultimate goals or motives.

The Three

were among the first dragons to walk the world. The Red is a living engine of destruction. The Blue is a sorceress, perhaps even the original mother of all sorcery. The Black is queen of shadows and assassins. Unlike the Great Gold Wyrm, who must fight alone, the Three have learned to join forces.